Risk Management, Sustainability and Leadership

Edited by Larisa Ivascu,
Ben-Oni Ardelean and Muddassar Sarfraz

Published in London, United Kingdom

Risk Management, Sustainability and Leadership
http://dx.doi.org/10.5772/intechopen.102301
Edited by Larisa Ivascu, Ben-Oni Ardelean and Muddassar Sarfraz

Contributors
Mahmoud Shahrokhi, Majid Vaziri Sarashk, Alain Bernard, Aman Kiniso, Mikhail Pomazanov, Thomas Wolter, Bolaji Abdulkadir Usman, Yaprak Akçay Zileli

First published in London, United Kingdom, 2023 by IntechOpen
IntechOpen is the global imprint of INTECHOPEN LIMITED, registered in England and Wales, registration number: 11086078, 5 Princes Gate Court, London, SW7 2QJ, United Kingdom

British Library Cataloguing-in-Publication Data
A catalogue record for this book is available from the British Library

Additional hard and PDF copies can be obtained from orders@intechopen.com

Risk Management, Sustainability and Leadership
Edited by Larisa Ivascu, Ben-Oni Ardelean and Muddassar Sarfraz
p. cm.
Print ISBN 978-1-83769-991-9
Online ISBN 978-1-83768-218-8
eBook (PDF) ISBN 978-1-83768-219-5

For EU product safety concerns:
IN TECH d.o.o., Prolaz Marije Krucifikse Kozulić 3, 51000 Rijeka, Croatia,
info@intechopen.com or visit our website at intechopen.com.

Meet the editors

Dr. Larisa Ivascu, BA, MBA, Ph.D., is a professor in the Faculty of Management in Production and Transportation, Department of Management, Politehnica University of Timisoara, Romania. She has more than 15 years of experience in programming, teaching, and research. Dr. Ivascu is the chair of the Entrepreneurship Office at Politehnica University of Timisoara, and director of the Research Center for Engineering and Management. She is the president of the scientific committee of the Academy of Political Leadership, and vice president of the Society for Ergonomics and Work Environment Management. She has published 9 books, 8 book chapters, and more than 220 academic research studies and articles. Dr. Ivascu is also a keynote speaker for various international and national events.

Dr. Ben-Oni Ardelean, Ph.D., is a member of the Romanian Parliament and has extensive academic and political experience. He has held several important positions over the years, including vice president of the Chamber of Deputies (2017–2018); senator of Romania (2012–2016) and secretary of the Romanian Senate (2016); vice president of the National Liberal Party; and a member of the North Atlantic Treaty Organization Parliamentary Assembly (NATO PA), the Parliamentary Assembly of the Council of Europe (PACE), the South Eastern European Cooperation Process Parliamentary Assembly (SEECP PA), and other organizations. He is recognized as a leading figure for human rights and freedom, organizing and speaking at conferences, televised debates and talk shows, and promoting a new leadership model among conservatives for post-Communist countries and around the world. He is the author of several books and numerous academic articles. Dr. Ardelean is concerned with supporting those in need, helping others to help themselves, and motivating people to live a life of purpose, love, and compassion.

Dr. Muddassar Sarfraz is an assistant professor at the School of Management, Zhejiang Shuren University, PR China. He completed a post-doctoral fellowship in business administration from the Business School of Hohai University, China. He has worked as a researcher and lecturer in various institutes and lectured on business research methods, business management, corporate social responsibility, business strategy, and strategic management. He has also attended several national and international conferences as a keynote speaker. He has published more than 120 papers in foreign authoritative journals and academic conferences at home and abroad. He is an associate and guest editor of several journals such as *Energies, International Journal of Work Organisation and Emotion, Etikonomi*, and *INQUIRY: The Journal of Health Care*

Organization, Provision, and Financing. He is an editorial board member of the *Journal of Chinese Human Resource Management* well as a member of the British Academy of Management, Chinese Economists Society, World Economic Association, and the American Economic Association, and an ambassador of the international MBA program, Chongqing University, PR China, for Pakistan.

Contents

Preface

Sustainability is an approach utilized by more and more organizations. In a dynamic environment, organizations approach the principles of sustainability and the circular economy. The transition from a linear economy to a circular economy implies the approach of principles, objectives, and goals of sustainability. We cannot talk about sustainability and development without efficient risk management. Risk management aims to develop an efficient organizational development environment through risk planning, assessment, analysis, and control. This process applies in all areas of activity and the evaluation framework is the same regardless of the field. This volume discusses methods, models, evaluation frameworks, benefits, barriers, and other dimensions of risk management.

Protecting the environment, streamlining the consumption of organizational resources, and reducing the amount of waste generated are some of the objectives of sustainability and circular economy efforts. The circular economy contributes to the sustainable development of a company or country and to the achievement of the global objectives of sustainable development. This book includes various studies on organizational and global sustainability.

Leadership has become a globally desirable approach that can help improve organizational competitiveness and reduce organizational risks. Risks and barriers in risk-free management can be well managed through effective organizational leadership. Leadership has several benefits for organizations, including improved organizational relations, motivating people, creating an organization adaptable to changes, identifying efficient processes, making intelligent decisions, and developing the organization over a long period of time. This book also explores different areas of leadership.

Furthermore, the book identifies strategic challenges for risk management, sustainability, and leadership, examines potential factors that affect business growth, and offers new opportunities for enterprises. It is organized into three main sections on risk management, sustainability, and leadership. It covers several important topics in the context of global sustainability and environmental dynamics:

- role of sustainability and corporate risk management
- relationship between environmental risk management and sustainable management
- new approaches and models of risk analysis
- risk management in different countries
- approaches towards risk management strategies in the short and long term

- development of risk management models using fuzzy logic
- addressing climate problems and other adjacent problems in some countries
- societal risks and their management methods
- critical success factors for risk practitioners' communication and leadership practices
- quality of risk management for a wide segment of retail lending

Chapter 1, "Risk Analysis, a Fuzzy Analytic Approach", introduces an analytic risk analysis approach by defining the danger, target zones, and effects of the barriers by geometric shapes.

Chapter 2, "Development of a Risk Management Model by the Fuzzy DEMATEL Method in the Evaluation of Authorized Certification Bodies", develops a new risk management model using the fuzzy DEMATEL method, which is one of the multicriteria decision-making methods, for authorized certification bodies to determine, evaluate, and measure risks, and plan the necessary preventive and corrective actions according to the results obtained.

Chapter 3, "Climate and Environmental Risk Action: A Call for Fresh Commitments to Adaptation and Resilience in West African Sub-Region", examines climate and other environmental problems that have created challenges to agriculture and food security, water resources, health, energy, and infrastructure development.

Chapter 4, "Sources of Social Risks and Risk Management Arrangements", examines the origins of societal risks, risk management arrangements, and methods for urging institutions to manage risk in Ethiopia. The result of the analysis indicates social risks faced by households caused by governance failures, institutional disincentives, elite's exploitations, and inefficiency.

Chapter 5, "Communication and Leadership for Improving ERM Effectiveness", focuses on Germany to factor out multiple country-specific risk management regulations and sociocultural variations. It contributes to an enhanced understanding of the means available for risk practitioners to increase enterprise risk management (ERM) effectiveness. Further, the study extends the literature on critical success factors for risk practitioners' communication and leadership practices.

Chapter 6, "Risk Management Tools to Improve the Efficiency of Lending to Retail Segments", discusses the issue of assessing the quality of risk management for a wide segment of retail lending (from consumer loans to loans for self-employed persons and small and medium-sized enterprises). The chapter substantiates a marginal formula for assessing the economic benefits of improving the discriminatory power of the models on which risk management is based.

This book is a useful resource for specialists in the field as well as researchers. It also offers a series of introductory aspects for those who want to learn the concepts of risk, sustainability, and leadership.

The editors would like to acknowledge the help of all those involved in this project. Without their support, this book would not have been possible. First, we thank the contributing authors for their time and expertise. Second, we wish to acknowledge the valuable contributions of the reviewers whose comments improved the quality, coherence, and content of each of the chapters.

Dr. Larisa Ivascu
Faculty of Management in Production and Transportation,
Politehnica University of Timisoara,
Timisoara, Romania

Dr. Ben-Oni Ardelean
Faculty of Baptist Theology,
University of Bucharest,
Baptist Theological Institute,
Bucharest, Romania

Dr. Muddassar Sarfraz
School of Management,
Zhejiang Shuren University,
Hangzhou, PR China

Section 1

Risk Management

Chapter 1

Risk Analysis, a Fuzzy Analytic Approach

Mahmoud Shahrokhi, Majid Vaziri Sarashk and Alain Bernard

Abstract

One of the challenges in designing industrial systems is integrating accident risk analysis with the other technical analysis tools. In the face of this challenge, this paper introduces an analytic approach to defining the occupational risk entities in computer-aided design software by visualizing the risk entities as geometric shapes. It uses energy/barrier analysis and the fuzzy set theory to model the protective role of barriers and infer the effects of harmful agents on humans and assets (targets). It defines dangers and targets presence zones by fuzzy sets, the so-called "fuzzy spaces" demonstrated as geometric profiles. The barriers affect these geometric profiles, and fuzzy union and intersection aggregate the effects of several dangers and protective measures. The model calculates the quantitative risk indexes for the various workplace points. The proposed model is adapted to evaluate the risk in the computer-aided design platform during the workplace simulation. An example illustrates the model application in a one-dimensional space.

Keywords: fuzzy theory, risk analysis, computer-aided design

1. Introduction

Järvinen et al. emphasized the potential of three-dimensional (3D) simulation models for implementing risk analysis without presenting any specific model [1]. Wang et al. developed an enhanced automated 3D visualization ergonomic analysis integrated with a proposed fuzzy logic-based joint-level ergonomic risk assessment methodology for work modification and workplace design [2]. Ojstersek et al. used the modeling and simulation method and ergonomic analyses in workplaces and presented potential opportunities for improving productivity and cost [3].

Despite many efforts, researchers have failed to develop practical risk management approaches in 3D platforms; implementing the new concurrent engineering approaches requires integrating safety-engineering techniques into the 3D design applications [4]. One of the significant challenges in this domain is the complexity of risk analysis due to the need to consider many system parameters that are very difficult to quantify. These parameters explain the characteristics of the harmful factors, their effect on vulnerable targets (humans, assets, and the environment), and the role of the safety barriers [5]. In the face of these challenges, this paper proposes an integrated risk analysis approach to develop the appropriate 3D risk analysis modeling tools for use through the design process by introducing geometric methods for modeling risk in computer-synthesized three-dimensional and virtual reality platforms.

Shahrokhi and Bernard use the "fuzzy space" concept to model danger zones, target presence zones, and physical and perceptual barriers by geometrical profiles [6]. This model visualizes and identifies the risk concentration points in the simulated workplace. The present paper uses fuzzy spaces to illustrate the risk distribution in the workplace and applies fuzzy operations to calculate a quantitative risk index.

2. Background

Risk is a function of the probability and the consequence of an unwanted top event in terms of possible damage to a target (i.e., property, environment, and people) [7]. Many researchers attempt to integrate risk analysis into computer-aided design applications. Määttä studied the applications of the virtual environment to analyze the safety of new designs in a steel factory [8]. Abshire and Barron review real-world applications of virtual maintenance and present the provided facilities using the virtual environment and digital prototypes for Failure Mode Effect Analysis (FMEA) during the design process [9]. Gallego et al. implemented an interesting geometric risk assessment method using the linguistic variables for occupancy degree and occupancy time to model the number of people exposed to a harmful agent (HA) [10]. Hendershot uses contour maps to calculate the risk by superposing the impact zones and population distribution for 11 regions [11].

Many efforts are taken to model barriers as an essential concept that, due to their variety, is very difficult to be modeled in geometric forms. The barrier concept was initially based on the successive works of domino theory back in the 1930s, Haddon in 1966 and Gibson in 1961, which developed the idea of an accident as an abnormal or unexpected release of energy [12]. It identifies and evaluates the associated hazards of the harmful agents [13]. Barrier analysis contributes to the energy analysis and represents the barrier as the protector of the target from dangers [14]. When avoiding or eliminating the dangerous agent and hazards is impossible, the designer adds a series of safety barriers to reduce the risk of the undesired outcomes to an acceptable level [15]. Polet and Zhang et al. state that the barriers prevent events or accidents, resurrect the target, and mitigate the severity of adverse consequences [16, 17]. Hollnagel distinguishes the protector and the preventive barriers. It defines a barrier as the "equipment, constructions, or rules that can stop the development of an accident" [18]. The same idea is the origin of the bow-tie diagram when categorizing the barrier effects by prevention and mitigation effects [19].

Tinmannsvik et al. modeled an accident that occurs by failing control barriers, controlling the hazards, and defense barriers that protect the target due to the transformation of the latent failures to the realized losses [20]. Fithri et al. conducted occupational safety and health risk analysis in manufacturing companies using FMEA and FTA methods [21]. The proposed model by Choe and Leite describes accident causation and improves accident investigation methods [22]. With construction domain knowledge, they offered a safety risk generation and control model representing the dynamic safety risk.

Despite many efforts, modeling the material and immaterial barriers reminds the fundamental challenges of modeling the risk in 3D computer applications.

Guimaraes and Lapa (a) and Guimarães and Lapa (b) used fuzzy inference systems to estimate risk priority numbers by aggregating the expert opinions in the failure mode and effects analysis (FMEA) method [23, 24]. Huang et al. developed a fuzzy set approach to integrating human error evaluation results in the event tree analysis [25]. Sadeghi et al. review the applications of design theories and methodologies and design tools and techniques to analyze and identify work situations to improve human safety in manufacturing system design [26]. Echeverri et al. (a) developed a design process's risk analysis models by considering technological and human factors and using essential functions and the production system's internal energy flow [27]. The proposed model integrated elements from the different design approach, considering cost, time, and performance, incorporating safety factors through energy functions and organizational rearrangements. Echeverri et al. (b) developed a multi-criteria design framework considering energy flow through components to characterize its behavior via Energetic Technical Functions [28]. Fargnoli reviewed the research addressing design for safety in the industrial context, focusing on those research approaches to integrate human factors within design activities [29]. He concluded that there is a research gap between theory and practice. He proposed a unified design for the safety process to support integrating human factors in design activities more practically.

The present paper introduces an analytic risk analysis approach by defining the danger, the target zones, and the effects of the barriers by geometric shapes.

3. Methodology

The presented method defines danger and target zones by fuzzy membership and probability density functions, illustrating them by geometric profiles in the 3D model.

3.1 Defining danger zones

A danger zone (DZ) is a portion of space where a harmful event may occur [10]. Shahrokhi and Bernard define fuzzy space to calculate every point x's membership in the danger zone [6]. According to the fuzzy sets notification, the following formula uses the integral and division symbols to explain that $\widetilde{DZ}$ is a continuous fuzzy set and assigns membership $\mu_{\widetilde{DZ}}$(x)to each x in the workplace.

$$\widetilde{DZ} = \int_x \frac{\mu_{\widetilde{DZ}}(x)}{x} \qquad 0 \le \mu_{\widetilde{DZ}}(x) \le 1 \quad \forall x \in X$$

As **Figure 1** presents, in contrast to the classic definition, a member (e.g., a point) is not just inside or outside of a fuzzy danger zone ($\widetilde{DZ}$); it may also have a degree of membership. Function $\mu_{\widetilde{DZ}}(x)$ indicates the membership of point x in danger zone $\widetilde{DZ}$.

Figure 2 illustrates a mono-dimensional danger zone and shows how a HA decreases by increasing the distance from the danger source.

A dangerous source can be an explosion, radiation, or a toxic gas leak. In all cases, a $\widetilde{DZ}$ assigns a membership value $\mu_{\widetilde{DZ}}(x)$ to each point, x. The $\widetilde{DZ}$ form is a function of the physical characteristics of the danger and the environmental conditions. For

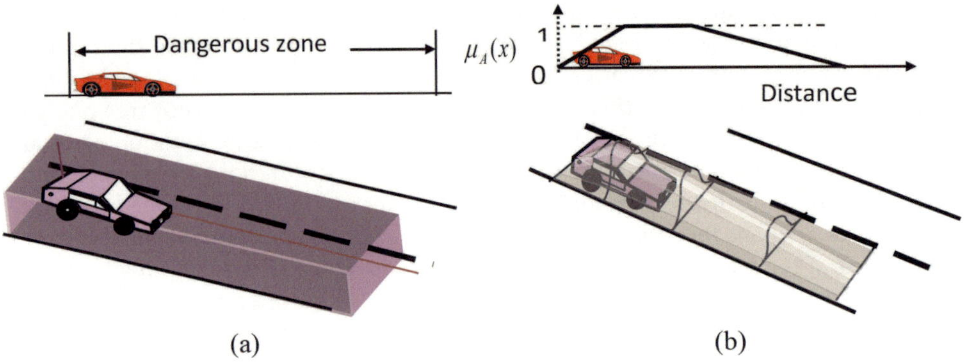

Figure 1.
Demonstration of the dangerous zone around a moving car using (a) the traditional and (b) the fuzzy space definitions [6].

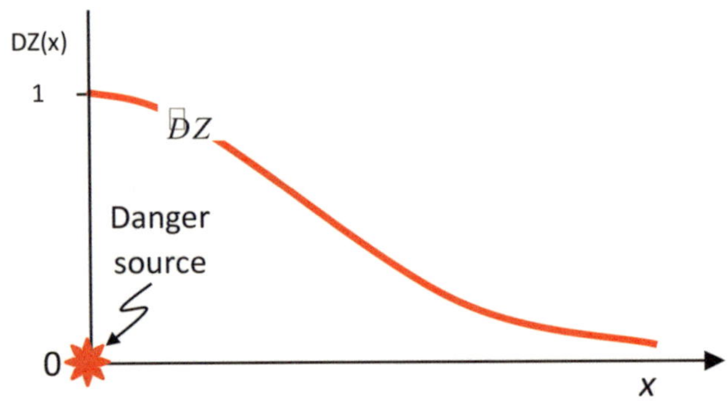

Figure 2.
Schematic demonstrations of a one-dimensional $\widetilde{DZ}$.

example, for a punctual radioactive material, the radiation in a uniform environment decreases proportionally to the distance squared from the danger source.

3.2 Aggregating several danger zones

Fuzzy union apples on several dangers to form a total danger zone, as follows:

$$\widetilde{DZ} = \bigcup_{i=1}^{n} \widetilde{DZ}_i$$

The selection of an appropriate union method among standard union (max(a,b)), bounded sum (min(1,a + b)), and other fuzzy union operations are essential to simulate the actual effect of accumulated dangers on the target.

3.3 Defining the target zone

A fuzzy target zone ($\widetilde{TZ}$) is also a fuzzy space, indicating the geographical distribution of the presence of the target:

$$\widetilde{TZ} = \int_x \frac{\mu_{\widetilde{TZ}}(x)}{x}$$

The $\mu_{\widetilde{TZ}}(x)$ is the normalized target population density (P(x)) or the target presence probability f(X) in point x. The following normalization formula converts the population density to a membership value by ensuring that the maximum membership value is 1:

$$\mu_{\widetilde{TZ}}(x) = \left(\frac{P(x)}{\underset{x}{Sup}(P(x))} \right)$$

It divides the population density of every point to their maximum (supremum) value for every x. For a target with random movement or stochastic existence, the model normalizes the probability function of the target presence, f(X), by using the following formula:

$$\mu_{\widetilde{TZ}}(x) = \left(\frac{f(x)}{\underset{x}{Sup}(f(x))} \right)$$

The membership function of TZ (i.e., $\mu_{\widetilde{TZ}}(x)$) indicates the distribution of the targets in the workplace. A fixed target creates a singleton fuzzy set target zone.

3.4 Modeling the barriers

The barriers limit danger and target zone(s) in several ways:

- Danger barriers ($\widetilde{DBs}$) impede or diminish the hazard's harmfulness and affected area by modifying $\widetilde{DZ}$.
- Target barriers ($\widetilde{TBs}$) modify $\widetilde{TZs}$ by impeding or decreasing the target membership in the danger zone or separating the target and HA by time.

The proposed approach models the above barriers by using geometric shapes. Fuzzy barriers (i.e., $\widetilde{TBs}$ and $\widetilde{DBs}$) illustrate the geographical distribution of barriers' capability to impede the danger and target presence.

3.5 Modeling danger barriers

Figure 3a–c exemplify danger barriers for the following cases, respectively:

a. A gas mask reduces 60% of danger harmfulness

b. A firewall that prevents 80% of the heat from passing through

c. A hazard neutralization system with a Gaussian local efficiency

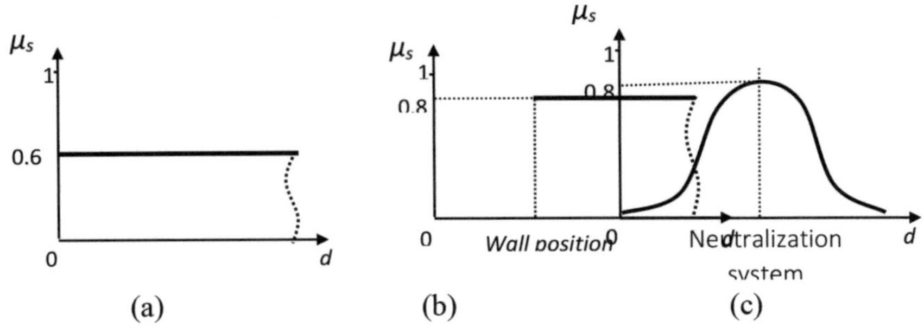

Figure 3.
Some schematic demonstration of danger barriers.

This approach uses fuzzy complement operation to transfer the danger barriers protection to danger barrier inefficiency ($\widetilde{DBI}$) as follows

$$\widetilde{DBI} = \neg\widetilde{DB} \qquad \mu_{\widetilde{DBI}}(x) = 1 - \mu_{\widetilde{DB}}(x) \qquad \forall x \in X$$

The risk exists when there is a danger and no barriers to neutralize the threat. Therefore, the practical (residual) danger zone equals the intersection of the original danger zone and the danger barrier inefficiency.

$$\widetilde{EDZ} = \widetilde{DZ} \cap \left(\neg\widetilde{DB}\right)$$

The following equation is applied when barrier effectiveness is proportional (e.g., using percentages). It means that the barrier reduces a specified portion of the danger.

$$\mu_{\widetilde{EDZ}}(x) = \mu_{\widetilde{DZ}}(x)\left(1 - \mu_{\widetilde{DB}}(x)\right) \qquad \forall x \in X$$

The following equation is valid when the barrier effectiveness is in absolute values (e.g., the barrier absorbs or filters a specified amount of the hazardous effects).

$$\mu_{\widetilde{EDZ}}(x) = Max\left(0, \mu_{\widetilde{DZ}}(x) - \left(1 - \mu_{\widetilde{DB}}(x)\right)\right) \qquad \forall x \in X$$

3.6 Modeling target barriers

The exemplified TBs affect the $\widetilde{TZ}$, For example, they may describe the following cases:

a detector, organizational measure or warning signs (**Figure 4a**), or a wall that prevents the presence of the target in a limited zone with specified reliability (**Figure 4b**), and a thermal protective cloth which controls 30% of the outside temperature from colliding with the wearer body (**Figure 4c**).

Some protective measures may affect both the $\widetilde{DZ}$ and $\widetilde{TZ}$ simultaneously; for example, **Figures 3b** and **4b** model effects of the same protection wall on the $\widetilde{DZ}$ and $\widetilde{TZ}$, respectively.

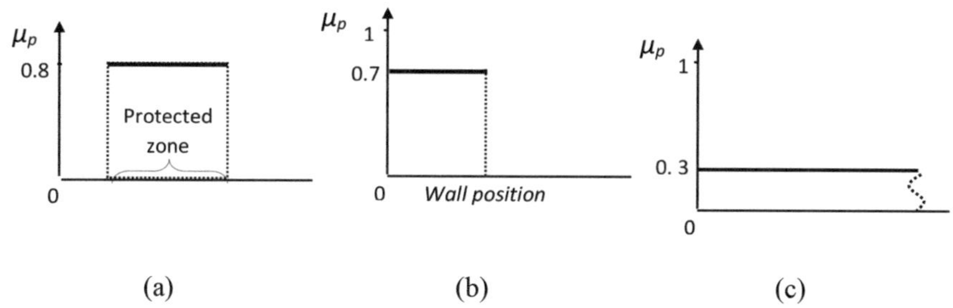

Figure 4.
Some schematic demonstration of target barriers.

3.7 Cumulative effects of several barriers

There are cumulative effects where two or several barriers are practical at the same place and time. The fuzzy union operator aggregates a set of J danger barriers and a set of K target barriers as effective danger barriers and practical target barriers, using the following formulas:

$$\widetilde{EDB}(x) = \bigcup_{j=1}^{J} \widetilde{DB}_j(x)$$

$$\widetilde{ETB} = \bigcup_{k=1}^{K} \widetilde{TB}_k$$

Fuzzy spaces $\widetilde{EDB}$ and $\widetilde{ETB}$ are the effective danger zone barrier and effective target barrier, respectively.

The definition of the fuzzy union in the above equations varies according to the cumulative barrier effects. The proposed approach defines serial and parallel barriers. In a serial barrier configuration, the danger must pass from all obstacles to impact the target (e.g., the consecutive antifire doors); in this case, the bounded sum (min(1, a + b)) is one of the appropriate s-norms if the danger reduced after passing from each barrier.

The standard union (i.e., max(a,b)) is a helpful s-norm when the most effective barrier is essential in limiting the danger zone or target presence zones.

In a parallel structure, it is sufficient for the threat to pass through one of the guards to impact the target. The analyst may consider the most unreliable barrier as the weakest link in the protection chain. A fuzzy intersection operator such as the standard intersection (e.g., min(a,b)) aggregates the parallel safety measures as effective danger follows:

$$\widetilde{EDB} = _{\cap} \widetilde{DB}_j$$

$$\widetilde{ETB} = _{\cap} \widetilde{TB}_k$$

3.8 Barriers inefficiency

Appling fuzzy compliment operator on "effective danger barriers" and "effective target barriers" results in "danger barriers inefficiency" and "target barriers inefficiency," respectively, as follows:

$$\widetilde{IDB} = \neg\widetilde{DB}$$

$$\widetilde{ITB} = \neg\widetilde{TB}$$

Operator ⌐ means fuzzy complement (fuzzy NOT) operation. The standard complement (⌐a = 1-a) is one of the most suitable fuzzy complementation methods. However, also there are other alternatives for this operator.

$$\mu_{\widetilde{IDB}}(x) = 1 - \mu_{\widetilde{DB}}(x) \qquad \forall x \in X$$

$$\mu_{\widetilde{ITB}}(x) = 1 - \mu_{\widetilde{TB}}(x) \qquad \forall x \in X$$

3.9 Apply barrier effects to the danger zone

Danger remains in dangerous places, but there is not enough protection; this means that the residual (effective) hazard at each point equals the intersection of the threat and the barriers inefficiency at that point. Therefore effective danger for every danger zone is:

$$\widetilde{EDZ} = \widetilde{DZ} \cap \widetilde{IDB}$$

In the same way, a practical target presence zone is:

$$\widetilde{ETZ} = \widetilde{TZ} \cap \widetilde{ITB}$$

Using the $\widetilde{EDZ}$ and $\widetilde{ETZ}$, the fuzzy risk zone is:

$$\widetilde{RZ} = \widetilde{EDZ} \cap \widetilde{ETZ}$$

In this case, multiplication is one of the alternatives for fuzzy intersection operation.

3.10 Determining the fuzzy risk zone

The proposed risk analysis approach uses the fundamentals of energy analysis and considers an accident resulting from the impact of a harmful agent (energy) on a target. Therefore, the fuzzy risk zone ($\widetilde{RZ}$)is an intersection area of a $\widetilde{DZ}$and a $\widetilde{TZ}$. The risk analyst should select the most appropriate fuzzy intersection operator (i.e., triangular norms (t-norm)) to reflect the accident consequence best. Triangular norms are indispensable for interpreting the conjunction in the intersection of fuzzy sets. One of the simplest choices is the product intersection, defined as:

$$\widetilde{RZ} = \widetilde{DZ} \cap \widetilde{TZ}$$

$$\mu_{\widetilde{RZ}}(x) = \mu_{\widetilde{DZ}}(x)\mu_{\widetilde{TZ}}(x) \qquad \forall x \in X$$

This formula uses the concept that the accident importance equals the multiplication of the hazard amplitude and the target presence probability or density. Other t-norms may be more appropriate for specific cases.

Figure 5 illustrates the distribution of targets in the neighborhood of a supposed hazard source.

Figure 6a shows both $\widetilde{DZ}$ and $\widetilde{TZ}$, and **Figure 6b** illustrates the resulting risk zone using the algebraic product t-norm as the fuzzy intersection operator. The horizontal axis corresponds to the distance from the hazard source. The vertical axis illustrates the risk index function; thus, risk zone $(\widetilde{RZ})$ presents the geographic distribution of the risk amplitude.

If the hazardous effects of several dangers are not similar, $\widetilde{RZ}$ should be calculated separately for different hazards.

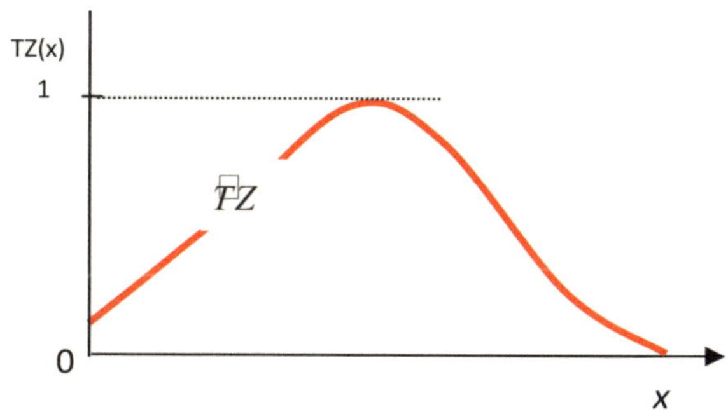

Figure 5.
Schematic demonstrations of a one-dimensional $\widetilde{TZ}$.

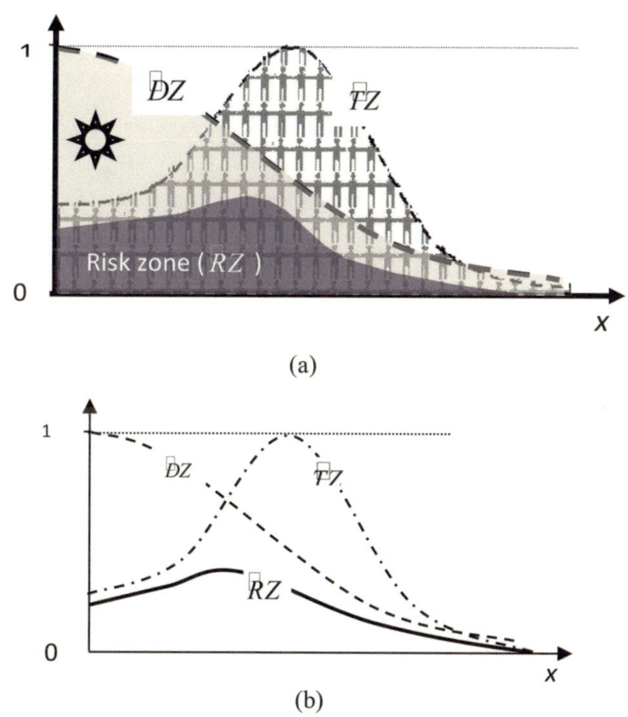

Figure 6.
Schematic demonstrations of one-dimensional $\widetilde{DZ}$, $\widetilde{TZ}$, and $\widetilde{RZ}$.

4. Examples

This section presents a numerical example using fuzzy discrete sets.

4.1 Numerical example

Suppose three similar dangers produce danger zones DZ1 to DZ3, limited by three serial danger barriers DB1 to DB3 with the following parameters (**Tables 1** and **2**):

Because the danger barriers are supposed on serial, the model accumulates their effects. For this example, using bounded sum fuzzy union $(\mu_{\widetilde{DB_1} \oplus \widetilde{DB_2}}(x) = \min\left(1, \mu_{\widetilde{DB_1}}(x) + \mu_{\widetilde{DB_2}}(x)\right))$, the effective danger barrier is:

Therefore, the danger barriers inefficiency zones are (**Table 3**).

Suppose the barriers reduce some specific proportion of the danger, so the residual danger zones after applying the above barriers, by using $\widetilde{EDZ} = \widetilde{DZ} \cap \widetilde{IDB}$ and the Algebraic product $(\mu_{\widetilde{EDZ}}(x) = \mu_{\widetilde{DZ}}(x)\mu_{\widetilde{IDB}}(x))$ intersection are (**Table 4**).

Consider 4 targets, using the following protective barriers for targets T1 to T4 (**Table 5**).

The above values indicate the protectives proportion of targets barriers used by different targets in different places. Using the fuzzy complement, the Inefficiency of the above protective measures is (**Table 6**).

The impacted dangers 1 to 3 to target 1, to target 1, after applying target barrier 1 is (**Table 7**).

In the above table, the model uses the bounded sum union to calculate the accumulated danger in each position.

In the same way, the total impacted danger for all the targets is (**Table 8**).

Parameter	**Parameter description**	**Values**					
x	**One-dimensional coordinates (x)**	**0**	**1**	2	3	4	5
$\mu_{\widetilde{DZ_1}}(x)$	Membership of x in DZ1	1	0.8	0.6	0.4	0.2	0.1
$\mu_{\widetilde{DZ_2}}(x)$	Membership of x in DZ2	0.8	0.9	1	0.5	0.4	0.1
$\mu_{\widetilde{DZ_3}}(x)$	Membership of x in DZ3	0.2	0.6	0.8	0.8	0.5	0.4
$\mu_{\widetilde{DB_1}}(x)$	Membership of x in DB1	0.1	0.2	0.3	0.2	0.1	0.1
$\mu_{\widetilde{DB_2}}(x)$	Membership of x in DB2	0.1	0.1	0.1	0.1	0.1	0.1
$\mu_{\widetilde{DB_3}}(x)$	Membership of x in DB3	0.0	0.0	0.2	0.0	0.0	0.0

Table 1.
The risk entities parameters.

x	**One-dimensional coordinates (x)**	**0**	**1**	**2**	**3**	**4**	**5**
$\mu_{\widetilde{EDB}}(x)$	Membership in Effective Danger Barrier	0.2	0.3	0.6	0.3	0.2	0.2

Table 2.
Membership of different coordinates in effective danger barriers fuzzy set.

DOI: http://dx.doi.org/10.5772/intechopen.108535

x	One-dimensional coordinate (x)	0	1	2	3	4	5
$\mu_{\widetilde{IDB}}(x)$	Membership in Danger Barriers Inefficiency	0.8	0.7	0.4	0.7	0.8	0.8

Table 3.
Membership of different coordinates in effective danger barrier inefficiency fuzzy set.

x	One-dimensional coordinates (x)	0	1	2	3	4	5
$\mu_{\widetilde{EDZ}_1}(x)$	Membership in Residual DZ1	0.8	0.56	0.24	0.28	0.16	0.08
$\mu_{\widetilde{EDZ}_2}(x)$	Membership in Residual DZ2	0.64	0.63	0.4	0.35	0.32	0.08
$\mu_{\widetilde{EDZ}_3}(x)$	Membership in Residual DZ3	0.16	0.42	0.32	0.56	0.4	0.32

Table 4.
Membership of different coordinates in residual fuzzy danger zones.

x	One-dimensional coordinate (x)	0	1	2	3	4	5
$\mu_{\widetilde{TB}_1}(x)$	Target Barrier effect, used by T1	0.2	0.2	0.2	0.2	0.2	0.2
$\mu_{\widetilde{TB}_2}(x)$	Target Barrier effect, used by T2	0.3	0.3	0.3	0.2	0.1	0.1
$\mu_{\widetilde{TB}_3}(x)$	Target Barrier effect, used by T3	0.4	0.4	0.4	0.4	0.4	0.4
$\mu_{\widetilde{TB}_4}(x)$	Target Barrier effect, used by T4	0.1	0.1	0.1	0.1	0.1	0.1

Table 5.
Membership of different coordinates in fuzzy target barriers.

x	One-dimensional coordinates (x)	0	1	2	3	4	5
$\mu_{\neg\widetilde{TB}_1}(x)$	Inefficiency of target barrier 1	0.8	0.8	0.8	0.8	0.8	0.8
$\mu_{\neg\widetilde{TB}_2}(x)$	Inefficiency of target barrier 2	0.7	0.7	0.7	0.8	0.9	0.9
$\mu_{\neg\widetilde{TB}_3}(x)$	Inefficiency of target barrier 3	0.6	0.6	0.6	0.6	0.6	0.6
$\mu_{\neg\widetilde{TB}_4}(x)$	Inefficiency of target barrier 4	0.9	0.9	0.9	0.9	0.9	0.9

Table 6.
Membership of different coordinates in residual fuzzy target barriers Inefficiency.

x	One-dimensional coordinates (x)	0	1	2	3	4	5
$\mu_{\widetilde{EDZ}_1^1}(x)$	T1 membership in Residual FDZ1	0.64	0.448	0.192	0.224	0.128	0.064
$\mu_{\widetilde{EDZ}_1^2}(x)$	T1 membership in Residual FDZ 2	0.512	0.504	0.32	0.28	0.256	0.064
$\mu_{\widetilde{EDZ}_1^3}(x)$	T1 membership in Residual FDZ 3	0.128	0.336	0.256	0.256	0.32	0.256
	Membership in Total Danger Zone for T1	1	1	0.768	0.76	0.704	0.384

Table 7.
Membership of different coordinates in residual fuzzy danger zones.

x	One-dimensional coordinates (x)	0	1	2	3	4	5
	T1 Membership in Total Danger Zone	1	1	0.768	0.76	0.704	0.384
	T2 Membership in Total Danger Zone	1	1	0.672	0.76	0.792	0.432
	T3 Membership in Total Danger Zone	0.96	0.966	0.576	0.57	0.528	0.288
	T4 Membership in Total Danger Zone	1	1	0.864	0.855	0.792	0.432

Table 8.
Membership of different coordinates in total fuzzy danger zones.

Suppose the position of the targets is a random variable with the following 132probabilities (**Table 9**).

Therefore the total risk for every target at each position is (**Table 10**).

The following figure shows the distribution of the danger (**Figure** 7).

The above chart shows that the most dangerous place is point 2, with a total risk index of 1.382, and particularly the risk for target 4 is very high at this point.

In the continue consider a target presence barrier with the following reliabilities (**Table 11**).

It impedes particularly the targets presented in point 2. The Inefficiency of this barrier is (**Table 12**).

Using algebraic product fuzzy intersection, the presence probability of the targets is (**Table 13**).

By applying algebraic product fuzzy intersection on target presence probability and targets membership in danger zones, the total risk for the targets is (**Table 14**).

The following chart illustrates the risk after applying this barrier (**Figure 8**).

The results indicate a reduction in the risk significantly.

x	One-dimensional coordinates (x)	0	1	2	3	4	5
$P_1(x)$	Presence probability of T1	0	0.1	0.2	0.3	0.2	0.3
$P_2(x)$	Presence probability of T2	0.1	0.2	0.2	0.2	0.3	0
$P_3(x)$	Presence probability of T3	0	0	0.4	0.5	0.1	0
$P_4(x)$	Presence probability of T4	0	0	1	0	0	0

Table 9.
Presence probability of targets in different coordinates.

x	One-dimensional coordinates (x)	0	1	2	3	4	5
$\widetilde{RZ}_1(x)$	Total risk for T1	0	0.1	0.154	0.228	0.141	0.115
$\widetilde{RZ}_2(x)$	Total risk for T2	0.1	0.2	0.134	0.152	0.238	0
$\widetilde{RZ}_3(x)$	Total risk for T3	0	0	0.230	0.285	0.053	0
$\widetilde{RZ}_4(x)$	Total risk for T4	0	0	0.864	0	0	0
$\widetilde{RZ}(x)$	Total risk	0.1	0.3	1.382	0.665	0.431	0.115

Table 10.
Total risk for targets in different coordinates.

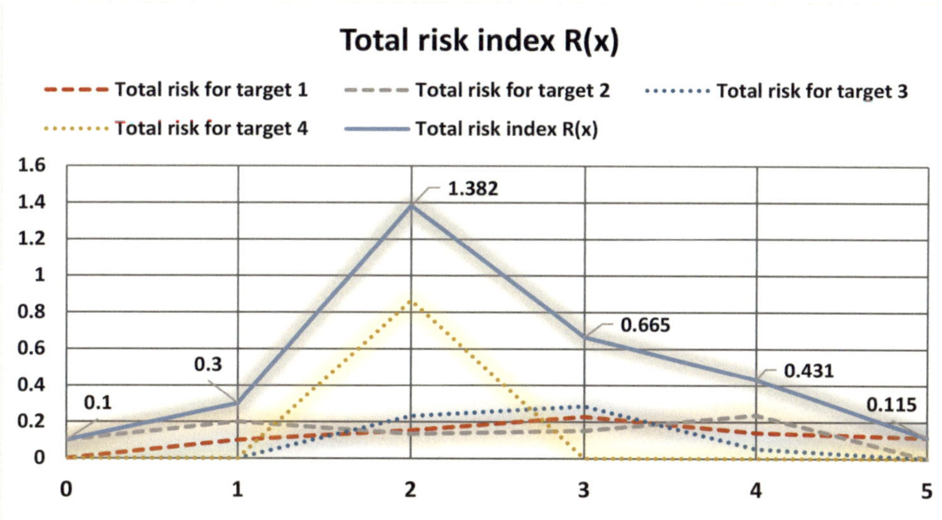

Figure 7.
The distribution of the risk for the targets.

x	One-dimensional coordinate (x)	0	1	2	3	4	5
$P_1(x)$	The presence barrier reliability for T1	0	0.1	0.3	0.1	0.1	0
$P_2(x)$	The presence barrier reliability for T2	0	0	0.2	0.2	0.2	0
$P_3(x)$	The presence barrier reliability for T3	0	0	0.4	0.1	0.1	0
$P_4(x)$	The presence barrier reliability for T4	0	0	0.8	0	0	0

Table 11.
The effects of presence barriers for targets in different coordinates.

x	One-dimensional coordinates (x)	0	1	2	3	4	5
$P_1(x)$	The presence barrier inefficiency for T1	1	0.9	0.7	0.9	0.9	1
$P_2(x)$	The presence barrier inefficiency for T2	1	1	0.8	0.8	0.8	1
$P_3(x)$	The presence barrier inefficiency for T3	1	1	0.6	0.9	0.9	1
$P_4(x)$	The presence barrier inefficiency for T4	1	1	0.2	1	1	1

Table 12.
The effects of presence barriers Inefficiency for targets in different coordinates

x	One-dimensional coordinates (x)	0	1	2	3	4	5
$P_1(x)$	Modified presence probability of T1	0	0.09	0.14	0.27	0.18	0.3
$P_2(x)$	Modified presence probability of T2	0.1	0.2	0.16	0.16	0.24	0
$P_3(x)$	Modified presence probability of T3	0	0	0.24	0.45	0.09	0
$P_4(x)$	Modified presence probability of T4	0	0	0.2	0	0	0

Table 13.
The modified presence probability of targets in different coordinates.

x	One-dimensional coordinates (x)	0	1	2	3	4	5
$\widetilde{RZ}_1(x)$	Total risk for T1	0	0.09	0.108	0.205	0.127	0.115
$\widetilde{RZ}_2(x)$	Total risk for T2	0.1	0.2	0.108	0.122	0.190	0
$\widetilde{RZ}_3(x)$	Total risk for T3	0	0	0.138	0.257	0.048	0
$\widetilde{RZ}_4(x)$	Total risk for T4	0	0	0.173	0	0	0
$\widetilde{RZ}(x)$	**Total risk**	0.1	0.29	0.526	0.583	0.364	0.115

Table 14.
The total risk for targets in different coordinates.

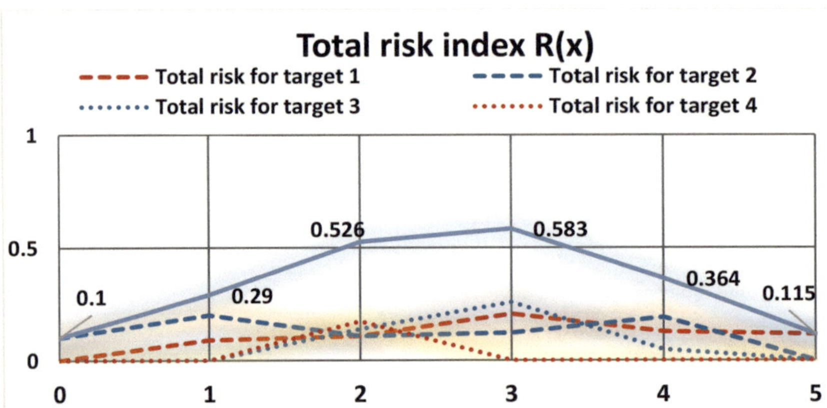

Figure 8.
The distribution of the risk for the targets, after applying the presence target.

5. Discussion

The proposed fuzzy analytical approach attempts to simplify the complexity of the traditional risk analysis by demonstrating the geometric profiles of risk analysis entities. This method models dangers, target presence, material, and immaterial barriers and provides a communication/analysis tool in graphical design platforms.

By using this approach in simulation applications, danger, target, and value attributes may vary during the simulated period. For instance, the magnitude of the HA and target position may vary according to the target and HA position. A software may calculate these parameters for each of the simulation sequences separately. The duration of simulation sequences is essential for calculating a total risk index for a simulated operation.

Shahrokhi and Bernard (2006) presented more discussion about the target vulnerability and worth. An event tree analysis may calculate the probability of occurrence of the simulated conditions. Defining the danger zone and target presence zone provided an index for quantitative risk analysis. The quantitative approaches require carefully scaling factors. For a fixed target, the presence zone will have infinite amplitude. The adaptability of fuzzy operations provides excellent flexibility to tailor the model according to typical situations. The method improves by considering several risks for a group of targets by applying fuzzy operations. Though the impact mode, including the impact duration and direction, is fundamental to estimating the accident severities, authors believe that in many risk analysis methods, including energy/barrier analysis, the assumptions related to the impact mode are not robust and sufficient.

Most of the barriers have not only protection effects; they relocate or reform DZ or TZ. For example, a protection wall increases the concentration of the DZ and TZ in a limited space.

Other fuzzy union operators can model the modification of the DZ/TZ by the barriers.

This model assumes a linear relationship between the damage and impact time because the presence zone demonstrates the duration of the target presence at each point. However, by defining the presence zone as the population density, the model ignores each target impact time. Like many other risk analysis methods, there is no assumption about other impact mode attributes. Therefore, the model's validity depends on the system's specifications. The model considers the danger zone as a stable and fixed region. In this case, the fundamentals theories are valid only for separated sequence times. A moving and dynamic danger zone is more appropriate if the danger source's harmfulness or position is unstable. Shahrokhi and Bernard (2006) discussed this case.

This model is applicable for calculating the cumulative risk indexes for a group of targets and hazards.

6. Conclusion

This paper presents a graphical approach to explain the geographical distribution of the danger and target presence to show the results of scientific calculations, experts' opinions, and observations. Using geographical risk attributes instead of their simple values provides a spatial risk analysis approach to present the workplace's danger concentration points and neighborhoods. The model introduces a geometric definition for the probability and severity of the professional risk and material/immaterial barriers using the fuzzy space concept. This definition lets to separate the barriers' severity and probability effects and use the fuzzy set operations to determine the risk and barrier effects. It assigns a risk membership to each workplace location and aggregates all points to provide a total risk index. The model is appropriate for calculating the cumulative risk indexes for a group of targets and hazards.

Author details

Mahmoud Shahrokhi[1*], Majid Vaziri Sarashk[2] and Alain Bernard[3]

1 University of Kurdistan, Sanandaj, Iran

2 Department of Industrial Engineering, Najafabad Branch, Islamic Azad University, Najafabad, Iran

3 Laboratoire IRCCyN, Ecole centrale de Nantes, Nantes, France

*Address all correspondence to: shahrokhi292@yahoo.com

References

[1] Järvinen J, Kuivanen R, Viitaniemi J. Safety design by using three-dimensional simulation models. International Journal of Industrial Ergonomics. 1996;**17**(4): 343-350

[2] Wang J, Li X, Han S, Al-Hussein M. Construction workers' behavior assessment using 3D visualization and fuzzy logic method. In: Intelligent Construction and Sustainable Buildings 2020 Oct 14. Reston, VA: American Society of Civil Engineers; 2020. pp. 47-54

[3] Ojstersek R, Buchmeister B, Vujica HN. Use of data-driven simulation Modeling and visual computing methods for workplace evaluation. Applied Sciences. 2020; **10**(20):7037

[4] Shahrokhi M, Bernard A. A fuzzy accident risk analysis approach for a concurrent engineering platform. In: IFIP International Conference on Advances in Production Management Systems. Cham: Springer; 2021. pp. 351-360

[5] De Ru WG, Eloff JH. Risk analysis modelling with the use of fuzzy logic. Computers & Security. 1996;**15**(3): 239-248

[6] Shahrokhi M, Bernard A. A fuzzy approach for definition of dangerous zone in industrial systems. In: 2004 IEEE International Conference on Systems, Man and Cybernetics (IEEE Cat. No. 04CH37583). The Hague, Netherlands: IEEE; 10 October 2004;7:6318-6324. DOI: 10.1109/ICSMC.2004.1401392

[7] Jo YD, Park KS. Dynamic management of human error to reduce total risk. Journal of Loss Prevention in the Process Industries. 2003;**16**(4):313-321

[8] Määttä T. Virtual Environments in Machinery Safety Analysis. VTT Technical Research Centre of Finland; VTT Publications. 2003. Vol. 516. p. 170. Available from: https://publications.vtt.fi/pdf/publications/2003/P516.pdf

[9] Abshire KJ, Barron MK. Virtual maintenance real-world applications within virtual environments. In: Annual Reliability and Maintainability Symposium. 1998 Proceedings. International Symposium on Product Quality and Integrity. Anaheim, CA, USA: IEEE; 1998. pp. 132-137. DOI: 10.1109/RAMS.1998.653690

[10] Gallego LE, Duarte O, Torres H, Vargas M, Montana J, Pérez E, et al. Lightning risk assessment using fuzzy logic. Journal of Electrostatics. 2004; **60**(2–4):233-239

[11] Hendershot DC. A simple problem to explain and clarify the principles of risk calculation. In: International Conference and Workshop on Risk Analysis in Process Safety. Bristol, UK: Rohm and Haas Company; 1997; Available online: http://citeseerx.ist.psu.edu/viewdoc/summary?doi=10.1.1.124.7084

[12] Livingston AD, Jackson G, Priestley K. Root causes analysis: Literature review. HSE Contract Research. 2001. p. 53

[13] Harms-Ringdahl L. Assessing safety functions—Results from a case study at an industrial workplace. Safety Science. 2003;**41**(8):701-720

[14] Guldenmund F, Hale A, Goossens L, Betten J, Duijm NJ. The development of an audit technique to assess the quality of safety barrier management. Journal of Hazardous Materials. 2006;**130**(3):234-241

[15] Trost WA, Nertney RJ. Barrier Analysis. US Department of Energy; Ref. DOE 76-45/29, SSDC-29; 1995. p. 34

[16] Polet P. Modélisation des franchissements de barrières pour l'analyse des risques des systèmes homme-machine (Doctoral dissertation, Valenciennes)

[17] Zhang Z, Chaali A, Vanderhaegen F. A Comparative Study on Prediction of Human Operator Violation Using Neural Networks. In: 2004 IEEE International Conference on Systems, Man and Cybernetics. The Hague, Netherlands: IEEE; 10 October 2004;**3**:2599-2604. DOI: 10.1109/ICSMC.2004.1400722

[18] Hollnagel E. Accident Analysis and Barrier Functions. Project TRAIN; Feb. 1999. Available from: https://www.researchgate.net/publication/251559941

[19] De Dianous V, Fiévez C. ARAMIS project: A more explicit demonstration of risk control through the use of bow–tie diagrams and the evaluation of safety barrier performance. Journal of Hazardous Materials. 2006;**130**(3):220-233

[20] Tinmannsvik R, Sklet S, Jersin E. Investigation methodology: Man, technology, organisation (in Norwegian only). SINTEF. October 2005. Report no.: STF38 A04422. Available from: http://www.ptil.no/NR/rdonlyres/63D64078–11AA–4AC7–931FA6A6CB790573/0/UlykkesgranskingSTF38A04422.pdf

[21] Fithri P, Hasan A, Kurnia I. Risk analysis for occupational safety and health in manufacturing company using FMEA and FTA methods: A case study. In: IOP Conference Series: Materials Science and Engineering. 2020. IOP Publishing; 1 December 2020;**1003**(1):012073. DOI: 10.1088/1757-899x/1003/1/012073

[22] Choe S, Leite F. Transforming inherent safety risk in the construction industry: A safety risk generation and control model. Safety science. 2020;**124**:104594

[23] Guimaraes AC, Lapa CM. Effects analysis fuzzy inference system in nuclear problems using approximate reasoning. Annals of Nuclear Energy. 2004;**31**(1):107-115

[24] Guimarães AC, Lapa CM. Fuzzy FMEA applied to PWR chemical and volume control system. Progress in Nuclear Energy. 2004;**44**(3):191-213

[25] Huang D, Chen T, Wang MJ. A fuzzy set approach for event tree analysis. Fuzzy Sets and Systems. 2001;**118**(1):153-165

[26] Sadeghi L, Dantan JY, Siadat A, Marsot J. Design for human safety in manufacturing systems: Applications of design theories, methodologies, tools and techniques. Journal of Engineering Design. 2016;**27**(12):844-877

[27] Echeverri JC, Dantan JY, Godot X. Integrated design–multi-view approach for production systems design. Procedia CIRP. 2021;**100**:217-222

[28] Echeverri JC, Dantan JY, Godot X. Design framework for production systems based on BES model–application in design for safety. Procedia CIRP. 2021;**99**:484-489

[29] Fargnoli M. Design for safety and human factors in industrial engineering: A review towards a unified framework. In: Proceedings of the 11th Annual International Conference on Industrial Engineering and Operations Management. Singapore; 2021. pp. 7-11

Chapter 2

Development of a Risk Management Model by the Fuzzy DEMATEL Method in the Evaluation of Authorized Certification Bodies

Yaprak Akçay Zileli

Abstract

The concept of risk, which has been seen as a danger for many years, has started to be seen as an opportunity today, and with this approach, risks have also begun to be considered as opportunities that can facilitate reaching goals. For these reasons, it is gaining importance day by day for businesses to adopt an effective risk management approach, to identify risks, to determine the degree of importance of risks and to define the actions that can be taken against these risks. Within the scope of this section, the possible risks in the activities of the certification bodies authorized by Vocational Qualification Authority operating in Turkey to conduct assessment and certification in order to determine vocational competencies were determined, and the Fuzzy DEMATEL method, which is one of the Fuzzy Multi-Criteria Decision Making Methods, was used to determine the weights of the risks. A new risk management model has been designed to be used in the evaluation and management of possible risks of organizations by using the weights obtained was designed for the assessment and management of risks.

Keywords: risk management, Fuzzy Multi-Criteria Decision Making Method, fuzzy DEMATEL method

1. Introduction

Determining all risks that businesses are exposed to, evaluating these risks, and planning preventive actions against these risks play an important role in achieving a sustainable competitive advantage and improving business performance. The modern risk management approach has strategic importance as it manages all risks and adopts a holistic approach in the context of the survival of the businesses [1]. Risk management gains special importance in being prepared for changing business conditions, managing change effectively, and minimizing the negative effects of uncertainties on the objectives of the enterprises while increasing their positive effects.

Vocational Qualifications Authority (VQA) is a public institution with administrative and financial autonomy established in Turkey in order to establish and operate a national qualification system compatible with the European Union. The national occupational standards of the occupations performed in Turkey are prepared by the Vocational Qualifications Authority and also national qualification documents that design the assessment and certification processes to be carried out in order to determine the competent individuals in the relevant occupation based on the occupational standards are developed. Both occupational standards and qualifications documents are developed according to needs of sectors in cooperation with sector institutions. Assessment and certification processes are operated through the certification bodies authorized by VQA in accordance with national qualification documents [2].

Certification bodies authorized by VQA are for-profit organizations, and their financial sustainability is among the authorization conditions. These institutions are required to be accredited according to the "ISO 17024 Conformity assessment – General requirements for bodies operating certification of persons" and meet the authorization conditions determined by VQA [3]. Within the scope of the authorization conditions, these institutions regarding risk management evaluate their assessment activities and define, measure, and evaluate their risks in a way to eliminate uncertainties in the realization of their objectives and in the effective implementation of their procedures and to carry out the necessary preventive actions to prevent these risks [3].

In this context, a new risk management model has been designed and proposed by using the fuzzy DEMATEL method, which is one of the multi-criteria decision-making methods, in order for authorized certification bodies to determine their risks, evaluate and measure risks, and plan the necessary preventive and corrective actions according to the results obtained.

2. Risk and risk management

Although the concept of risk appears in the literature in two ways, traditional and new, in the traditional approach, risk is considered a negative concept and is expressed as a threat, danger, damage, or loss [4]. In the traditional approach, risks are handled independently from each other, focused on specific risks, and activities to reduce risk are continued [5].

In classical risk management, each unit in the business focuses on the risks that are directly affected, and in its area of interest, the focused risks are related to the financial dimension and other risks are not taken into account. Independent determination of the risk in other units, without considering the effects on the entire enterprise, prevents the formation of a risk policy adopted both among the units and throughout the enterprise [6].

In the modern approach, risk management is under the coordination of the senior manager, but under the responsibility of all units and employees, and not only limited to the financial dimension but also considers other risks. In this approach, which integrates with all employees and all processes of the enterprise, risk management exhibits an approach that is compatible with all goals and objectives of the enterprise [1].

Risk, which was seen as a danger for many years, can be seen as an opportunity today. Hazard is only the negative aspect of risk that can lead to undesirable consequences. Opportunity, on the other hand, is the probability of an event that positively affects the realization of business objectives, and it is aimed to create value and protect the value created with opportunities. Our age's risk management approach adopts a risk management approach that transforms risks into opportunities and thus increases value [7].

With the new approach, risks are evaluated by taking into account the entire enterprise, critical risks are primarily focused, the most appropriate response to risks is determined, and all employees take responsibility [5].

For this reason, while the concept of risk was defined as the negative effect of an unexpected event or uncertainty on targets in the early periods [8], with the new approach adopted in recent years, the negative side of risk was not only focused on but also aspects such as opportunity, profit, and gain, which express the positive aspects, were also discussed [4].

In this framework, the concept of risk is considered as threats, negativities that may prevent the realization of the objectives, or opportunities that may facilitate the achievement of the objectives [9, 10].

The Project Management Institute defines the concept of risk as "an event or condition with uncertainty that, if realized, could have a positive or negative impact on the objectives of the organization." According to the ISO 31000:2009 Principles and Principles standard risk, it is explained as the effect of uncertainty on the targets, and with the effect expressed here, positive or negative deviations from the expected situation are expressed [11].

The concept of risk management was first used in the insurance field in the early 1950s. The first principles of risk management were developed in the early 1960s, and in this context, it was emphasized that risks should not be contented with only insurance, but all risks should be managed. In parallel with this, risk management started to play an active role in political, economic, military, scientific, and technological fields in the following years [7].

Risk management, which was applied only for insurable risks in the past, has gained a different dimension today. Businesses have started to implement risk management in a way that takes into account strategic, operational, and financial risks [12].

As external factors, while it is expressed as economic events, natural environmental events, political events, social events, and technological events, it is classified as infrastructure-related events, personnel-related events, process-related events, and technology-related events as internal factors [13].

While the risks faced by businesses are generally classified as being from strategic, financial, operational, and external environments, the classification system based on internal and external factors by COSO (Committee of Sponsored Organizations), which offers a widely accepted risk management framework, is one of the comprehensive classifications [13].

The activities for businesses to define their risks and evaluate and reduce their risks appear as risk management. According to ISO 31000, the risk management process includes communication, negotiation, scoping, assessing risks, responding to risks, monitoring, reviewing, recording, and reporting [14].

All activities carried out on this basis, with the identification and evaluation of events or situations that are likely to occur and which are considered to affect the achievement of the administration's goals and objectives, constitute the subject of risk management [15].

In summary, risk management exhibits a proactive approach that reduces uncertainties and the negative effects of uncertainty to a more acceptable level and prevents problems before they arise. In addition, it aims to lead the way in which opportunities are recognized in advance and turn them into advantages for the business.

Thanks to risk management, businesses identify the risks involved in the activities they carry out, evaluate the possibility of the risks to occur and the effect they will have when they occur, plan the necessary preventive actions, and thus turn the threat or danger element posed by the risks into an advantage [12]. With risk management, it is aimed not to completely eliminate risks, but to enable businesses to better understand their risks and manage them at a level they can control [16].

3. Certification bodies and risk factors

3.1 Certification bodies authorized by the vocational qualifications authority

Within the scope of our study, the risk factors of certification bodies authorized by the Vocational Qualifications Authority, a public institution in Turkey, are evaluated.

Vocational Qualifications Authority (VQA) is a public institution with a public legal personality, administrative and financial autonomy, established to establish and operate a national qualification system compatible with the European Union. The establishment purpose of the institution, as stated above, is to establish and operate a national qualification system compatible with the European Union [2].

In this context, VQA carries out work and procedures related to the preparation of national occupational standards, the development of national qualifications based on national or international occupational standards, the execution of activities for assessment and certification within the framework of national qualifications, and the regulation of the Turkish Qualifications Framework [2].

Within the scope of national occupational standards, the knowledge, skills, attitudes, and behaviors that must be possessed in order to perform a profession successfully, and the tasks, duties, and performance criteria that must be exhibited are defined. Within the scope of national qualifications prepared on the basis of national occupational standards, the procedures and principles for assessment and certification activities are determined [17].

Assessment and certification activities according to national qualifications are carried out by certification bodies authorized by VQA. The most basic condition of being a certification body authorized by VQA is to be accredited according to the international personnel certification standard called "TS EN ISO/IEC 17024:2012 Conformity Assessment - General Conditions for Personnel Certification Bodies". After accreditation, compliance with the conditions determined in VQA legislation and regulations is examined, audited, and evaluated. Institutions and organizations that meet the requirements are authorized by VQA and carry out assessment and certification activities in relevant national qualifications. These institutions and organizations are regularly audited through both programmed and unscheduled audits [18].

The criteria that authorized certification bodies must meet are defined in the scope of "Authorization Criteria and Implementation Guide for Certification Bodies". The criteria are grouped under 13 main headings. Each main criterion under these 13 main headings and sub-criteria related to this criterion define the conditions that must be met [3].

According to this guide, certification bodies must meet the conditions determined within the scope of legal status and organizational structure of organizations; human resources and management; physical, technical, and financial resources and management; examination materials, measurement, evaluation, and certification activities; internal and external verification; objections and complaints; information sharing;

communication and guidance; internal and external audit activities; management of objectivity; policy, and objectives; and management of documents and records [3].

Situations or events that may prevent the realization of these conditions appear as risks. In this respect, organizations are expected to evaluate all their procedures, including the steps to be followed in fulfilling these conditions, to identify and evaluate possible risks that may prevent the effective implementation of their procedures, and to implement the necessary preventive actions to prevent risks [3].

3.2 Risks in assessment and certification activities of certification bodies

Within the scope of the study, the risks used in the design of the model are considered as the risks arising from the assessment and certification activities of the organizations, the human resources, physical and technical resources used in these activities, internal verification activities, assessment materials, the impartiality and reliability of the assessment, and certification activities.

While determining the risks, they are defined as situations or events that may cause significant or major noncompliance if they occur within the organizations, and that may cause the suspension or cancelation of the authority of the institutions. The identified risks were also confirmed by an expert group consisting of lead auditors appointed by VQA to take part in the audits of the organizations. Risks have been determined under the main headings and the risks are listed in **Table 1** under the main headings.

The model designed in this study was used to evaluate the risks (**Table 1**) and it was proposed as a new risk assessment method.

4. Fuzzy DEMATEL (fuzzy decision-making trial and evaluation laboratory) method

The DEMATEL method is a multi-criteria decision-making method and is used to solve many complex problems. With this method, the relationships between the variables are evaluated and these relationships are visualized through diagrams showing cause-and-effect relationships. Thanks to this method, all variables are determined as influencing and affected variables, or in other words, cause-effect relationships and the structural relationship between the variables is revealed [19]. The DEMATEL method has a superior feature compared to other multi-criteria decision-making methods as it deals with the interrelationships between variables.

Fuzzy logic was first introduced by Lotfi A. Zadeh in 1965. Fuzzy logic is an approach that is based on thinking like a human and adopts that the key elements of human thought are linguistic variables [20]. The differences in perception arising from the way of thinking of people and the uncertainties in their subjective behaviors and goals are explained by the concept of blurriness, and in this respect, it is defined as the application of fuzzy mathematics to the real world. In fuzzy logic, variables are classified without precise evaluations. Unlike classical logic, it models the data by using linguistic variables such as "very little, little, medium, high, very high" instead of definite propositions such as true-false or yes-no. Afterward, these expressions are converted into fuzzy numbers and more realistic solutions are obtained [21].

The DEMATEL method reveals the relationship between variables in complex systems and it is not always possible to evaluate these variables with definite propositions. At this point, fuzzy logic is used and expert opinions about the variables are

Main risk group	Sub-risks
Human resources	Insufficient employment of assessors and internal verifiers.
	Failure of the assessor and internal verifiers to meet the assessor criteria.
	Assessors and internal verifiers do not have sufficient knowledge and experience.
	Lack of awareness of the assessor and internal verifiers about the system
Assessment and certification activities	The method used in theoretical and performance-based exams is not compatible with the qualifications.
	Failure to conduct theoretical and performance-based exams in accordance with the guidelines
	Assessor's failure to conduct exams in accordance with scenarios, checklists, and national qualifications
	Failure to perform assessment activities accurately, consistently, and reliably
	Failure to make correct, consistent, fair, and reliable certification decisions
Internal verification activities	Failure to operate internal verification activity for each national qualification, qualification unit, and assessor
	Failure to perform internal verification activities in accordance with national qualifications
	Failure of internal verifiers to make accurate, consistent, and fair assessments
	Inadequate creation of the sampling plan in internal verification activities
	Failure to take corrective actions for detected nonconformities within the scope of internal verification
Assessment material	Not creating enough questions to meet the knowledge statements in the annex of the qualification units
	The question booklets do not contain a sufficient number and quality of questions to meet the knowledge statements.
	Scenarios and checklists do not meet the skills and competencies in the annex of the qualification units
	Failure to verify the suitability of materials used in assessment processes
Physical and technical facilities	Inadequate physical environments to measure skills and competencies
	Failure to take adequate OHS measures in the areas where performance-based assessments are held
	Equipment and materials are not suitable for measuring skills and competencies
	Failure to take adequate measures to ensure the reliability of equipment
Impartiality and Reliability	Lack of awareness of assessor and internal verifiers for a consistent and fair assessment.
	Possible conflicts of interest between assessors and candidates
	The internal verifier has a conflict of interest with the candidate or assessor
	Failure to take adequate precautions for reliable assessment

Table 1.
Main risk group and sub-risks.

converted into fuzzy numbers. In summary, the Fuzzy DEMATEL method is obtained by transferring the DEMATEL method to the fuzzy environment [22].

When the studies in the literature with the fuzzy DEMATEL method are examined, the fuzzy DEMATEL method was used to investigate the factors affecting the adoption of new technology and to determine the relationship between the factors in the study conducted by Zargar et al. [23]. In the study by Chang et al., fuzzy DEMATEL method was used to determine supplier selection criteria [24]. In the study conducted by Chou et al., fuzzy AHP and fuzzy DEMATEL methods were applied integrated in order to evaluate human resources in the field of science and technology [25]. Çelik and Akyüz used the fuzzy DEMATEL method to evaluate the critical hazards in the gas release process in oil tankers [26]. Seker and Zavadskas used the fuzzy DEMATEL method in the analysis of occupational risks in the construction industry [27]. Mahmoudi et al. used the fuzzy DEMATEL method to determine the critical success factors for the self-care process in heart failure [28]. Feng and Ma determined the factors affecting service innovation in the manufacturing sector with fuzzy DEMATEL [29].

4.1 Steps of the method of fuzzy DEMATEL

Although the steps of the fuzzy DEMATEL method are similar to the steps of the DEMATEL method, fuzzy numbers are used in this method and these numbers need to be defuzzification in order to convert them into definite results. At this point, unlike the DEMATEL method, the defuzzification process is integrated into the steps of the method. Although various methods are used in defuzzification, the CFCS (Converting Fuzzy Data into Crisp Scores) method used in a study by Opricovic and Tzeng in 2003 was used within the scope of our study [30].

Zhou et al. used the fuzzy DEMATEL method to determine critical success factors in emergency management in 2011. The steps followed in the study by Zhou et al. are listed below [31]. In this study, Zhou et al. used the CFCS method, developed by Opricovic and Tzeng [30], which is used to defuzzifying fuzzy numbers. The steps and demonstrations presented within the scope of Zhou et al.'s work were also used in our study [31];

Step 1: Determine the initial direct-relation matrix.

At this stage, a group of experts is formed in order to determine the relationships between variables, criteria, or factors. Linguistic variables and fuzzy numbers in **Table 2** are used when group members make pairwise comparisons.

At this stage, the relations between the criteria or factors are evaluated by experts by making pairwise comparisons. As a result of the evaluation, an initial direct matrix consisting of triangular fuzzy numbers is obtained. Defuzzification processes are applied to obtain the initial direct matrix with the crisp values.

Step 2: Defuzzification.

In this study, CFCS (converting fuzzy data into crisp scores) method was used in order to convert fuzzy numbers into crisp values.

Definition	Triangular fuzzy numbers
No influence	(0, 0, 0.25)
Very low influence	(0, 0.25, 0.50)
Low influence	(0.25, 0.50, 0.75)
High influence	(0.50, 0.75, 1.00)
Very high influence	(0.75, 1.00, 1.00)

Table 2.
Triangular fuzzy numbers according to the degree of effect.

$$z^k_{ij} = (l_{ij}, m_{ij}, r_{ij}) \tag{1}$$

$1 \leq k \leq K$.
K: Number of experts.
z^k_{ij}: Evaluation of the effect of the i criterion on the j criterion by the kth expert in a fuzzy environment.

The following formulas are used for normalization, calculation of left and right normalized value, calculation of total normalized value, and calculation and integration of crisp value for defuzzification operations.

4.1.1 Normalization

$$xl^k_{ij} = \left(l^k_{ij} - \min_{1 \leq k \leq K} l^k_{ij}\right) / \Delta^{max}_{min}. \tag{2}$$

$$xm^k_{ij} = \left(m^k_{ij} - \min_{1 \leq k \leq K} l^k_{ij}\right) / \Delta^{max}_{min} \tag{3}$$

$$xr^k_{ij} = \left(r^k_{ij} - \min_{1 \leq k \leq K} l^k_{ij}\right) / \Delta^{max}_{min} \tag{4}$$

$$\Delta^{max}_{min} = max r^k_{ij} - \min l^k_{ij} \tag{5}$$

4.1.2 Computing of left (ls) and right (rs) normalized values

$$xls^k_{ij} = xm^k_{ij} / \left(1 + xm^k_{ij} - xl^k_{ij}\right) \tag{6}$$

$$xrs^k_{ij} = xr^k_{ij} / \left(1 + xr^k_{ij} - xm^k_{ij}\right) \tag{7}$$

4.1.3 Computing total normalized crisp values

$$x^k_{ij} = \left[xls^k_{ij}\left(1 - xls^k_{ij}\right) + xrs^k_{ij} xrs^k_{ij}\right] / \left(1 + xrs^k_{ij} - xls^k_{ij}\right) \tag{8}$$

4.1.4 Computing crisp values

$$BNP^k_{ij} = min l^k_{ij} + x^k_{ij} \Delta^{max}_{min} \tag{9}$$

4.1.5 Integrating crisp values

$$a^k_{ij} = \frac{1}{K} \sum\nolimits_k^{1 \leq k \leq K} BNP^k_{ij} \tag{10}$$

As a result of the operations performed, the initial direct-relation matrix is obtained.
Step 3: Obtaining the normalized direct-relation matrix
By means of the formula below, the normalized direct-relation matrix is obtained.

$$D = A/s \tag{11}$$

s = max (max $\sum_{j=1}^{n} aij$, max $\sum_{i=1}^{n} aij$)
i,j = 1,2, … … n
Step 4: Obtaining the total-relation matrix

When the normalized direct-relation matrix D is obtained, the total-relation matrix T is calculated using the formula below. "I" stands for the unit matrix

$$T = D + D^2 + D^3 + \dots \dots \dots = \sum_{i=1}^{\infty} D^i = D(I - D)^{-1} \tag{12}$$

Step 5: Identifying cause and effect groups

The sum of the rows in the T matrix is determined by ri and the sum of the columns by cj. Cause and effect groups are determined by calculating "ri – cj" and "ri + cj" values.

The "r" obtained as a result of row sums shows the effect of the ith factor on other factors. The sum of the columns "cj" shows the effect of other factors on the ith factor. "ri + cj" values show the total effect and the effective value of the relevant factor, in other words, the degree of relations with other criteria.

Among the "ri – cj" values, those with positive values express those that affect other criteria, while those with negative values express those who are affected by other criteria. In other words, the value of "ri – cj" expresses the effect of that criterion on the system [32].

Step 6: Producing diagrams of cause and effect groups

Diagrams are obtained by showing "ri + cj" values on the horizontal axis and "ri – cj" values on the vertical axis on the coordinate plane. If the (ri − cj) axis is positive, the factor is in the cause group. Otherwise, if the (ri − cj) axis is negative, the factor is in the effect group.

A threshold value is determined in order to get rid of the complexity of the criteria with a small effect level. The threshold value is determined by averaging the values in the total correlation matrix or by an expert group. The criteria below the threshold value are determined as the affected (effect) criteria, and the criteria above the threshold value are determined as the affecting (cause) criteria [33].

Step 7: Calculating criterion weights

The following formula was used to calculate the criterion weights [34].

$$w_i = \sqrt{[(r_i + c_j)]\ 2 + [(r_i - c_j)]\ 2} \tag{13}$$

$$\mathrm{Wi} = \frac{wi}{\sum_{i=1}^{n} wi}$$

Step 8: Operating the steps for the main criteria

All the steps described above are operated to determine the main criterion weights.

Step 9: Operating the steps for sub-criteria.

All the steps described above are operated for the sub-criteria under each main criterion group in order to calculate the sub-criteria weights, and as a result, the sub-criteria weights are calculated.

Step 10: Integrating main criterion and sub-criteria weights

The final weights are calculated by multiplying the weights of the main criteria with the weights of the sub-criteria.

5. Weighting the risks of authorized certification bodies by fuzzy DEMATEL method

Within the scope of the study, the main risks that may be encountered in certification bodies authorized by VQA and sub-risks related to these risks were determined, and these risks were confirmed by the lead auditors in the audit of certification bodies.

The weights of the risks were calculated using the "Fuzzy DEMATEL Method" introduced in the previous section.

Step 1: Demonstrating the relationship between risks

The network structure of the model is presented in the Figure below (**Figure 1**). The relations between the main criteria and the sub-criteria are shown in the network structure of the model. As a result of the evaluation made with the expert group, it was evaluated that all the criteria were in interaction with each other.

Step 2: Designing the questionnaire

A questionnaire consisting of two parts was designed for the application of the fuzzy DEMATEL method. In the first part of the questionnaire, in order to determine the relations between the main criteria, and in the second part, in order to determine the relations between the sub-criteria under each main criterion group, matrices were designed to allow pairwise comparison. Questionnaires were asked to make pairwise comparisons using these matrices and to determine whether the risks affect each other. The questionnaire was administered to a group of experts consisting of 12 people. The expert group was selected from people who are in charge as lead auditors in VQA audits and had sufficient knowledge and experience in assessment and certification and audit activities.

Step 3: Calculating the inconsistency rate of the questionnaire results

The inconsistency rate of the obtained data was determined in accordance with the formula for the calculation of the inconsistency rate presented within the scope of a study conducted by Wang and Tzeng in 2012 [35]. The formula is presented below;

$$\text{Inconsistency rate} = \frac{1}{n(n-1)} \sum_{i=1}^{n} \sum_{j=1}^{n} \frac{\left| a_{ij}^{p} - a_{ij}^{p-1} \right|}{a_{ij}^{p}} \times 100\% \qquad (14)$$

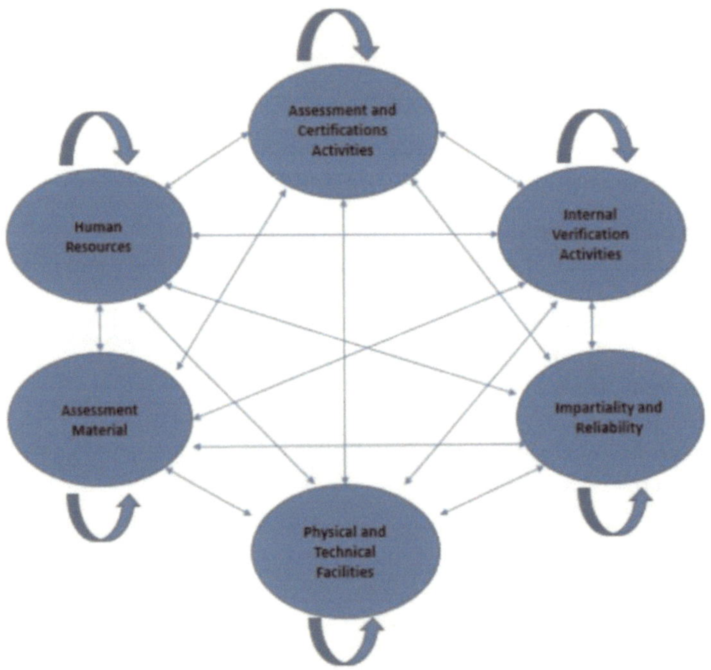

Figure 1.
Relations between main and sub-risk criteria.

n = Number of criteria
p = Number of experts

$$a_{ij}^{p} = \text{average of data from p experts for each pairwise comparison}$$

$$a_{ij}^{p-1} = \text{average of data from p} - 1 \text{ experts for each pairwise comparison}$$

If the inconsistency rate is <5%, the obtained data is determined to be consistent.

In line with the formula presented above, it has been determined that the data obtained as a result of the calculations made for the main criteria and the sub-criteria defined under the main criteria are consistent. Consistency rates are presented in **Table 3**. Since the consistency ratios of all criteria are less than 0.05, it is seen that the data are consistent.

Step 4: Conversion of survey data to fuzzy numbers

The data obtained as a result of pairwise comparisons made by each member of the expert group for the main criteria and sub-criteria were converted into fuzzy numbers. The triangular fuzzy values in **Table 1** were used to transform the data into fuzzy numbers.

Step 5: Utilizing CFCS (Converting Fuzzy Data into Crisp Scores) defuzzification method to defuzzifying fuzzy numbers and creating the initial matrix.

The normalization process was carried out by using the CFCS method steps presented in Eqs. (1)–(10). As a result of the calculations, xls and xrs matrices were obtained for both the main risk criteria group and the sub-risk criteria groups under

Criteria	Consistency rate	Evaluation
Main criteria	0,03	Consistent
Human resources	0,04	Consistent
Assessment and certification activities	0,03	Consistent
Internal verification activities	0,04	Consistent
Assessment material	0,04	Consistent
Physical and technical facilities	0,03	Consistent
Impartiality and reliability	0,04	Consistent

Table 3.
Consistency rate of the data obtained from the expert group for the main criteria and sub-criteria.

A matrix	1	2	3	4	5	6
1	0,045	0,980	0,898	0,568	0,431	0,841
2	0,586	0,045	0,630	0,668	0,508	0,768
3	0,610	0,790	0,045	0,610	0,553	0,648
4	0,357	0,941	0,633	0,045	0,567	0,645
5	0,240	0,770	0,594	0,568	0,045	0,513
6	0,703	0,907	0,785	0,575	0,497	0,045

Table 4.
Initial direct-relation matrix for main risk criteria (A).

the main risk criteria group. By using these matrices, the total normalized value and the crisp value were calculated.

After obtaining the crisp values, the initial direct-relation matrices were calculated using Eq. (10). The initial direct-relation matrix obtained for the main risk criteria is presented in **Table 4** for illustrative purposes. The same calculations were made for the sub-risk criteria groups.

Step 6: Obtaining the normalized direct-relation matrix

Normalized direct-relation matrices were obtained by using Eq. (11). The normalized matrix obtained for the main risk criteria is presented in **Table 5** for illustrative purposes. The same calculations were made for the sub-risk criteria groups.

Step 7: Obtaining the total-relation matrices

Using Eq. (12), the total-relation matrices were calculated. The total relation matrix obtained for the main risk criteria is presented in **Table 6**. Total relation matrices were also obtained for the sub-risk criteria groups.

Step 8: Identifying cause and effect groups

The sum of the rows in the T matrix is shown with ri and the sum of the columns with cj, and the cause and effect groups are determined by calculating the values of "ri – cj" and "ri + cj". The cause and effect groups calculated for the main risk criteria are presented in **Table 7**. Similarly, cause and effect groups were calculated for the sub-risk criteria groups.

A threshold value has been determined in order to avoid the complexity of the criteria with a small effect level. The threshold value was calculated by averaging the values in the total relationship matrix and 0.07 was obtained for the main risk criterion total relationship matrix.

D matrix	1	2	3	4	5	6
1	0,010	0,221	0,203	0,128	0,097	0,190
2	0,132	0,010	0,142	0,151	0,115	0,173
3	0,138	0,178	0,010	0,138	0,125	0,154
4	0,080	0,212	0,143	0,010	0,128	0,146
5	0,054	0,174	0,134	0,128	0,010	0,116
6	0,159	0,204	0,177	0,130	0,112	0,010

Table 5.
Normalized direct-relation matrix for main risk criteria (D).

T matrix	1	2	3	4	5	6
1	0,014	0,160	0,126	0,065	0,042	0,115
2	0,055	0,015	0,073	0,071	0,046	0,092
3	0,058	0,112	0,014	0,065	0,051	0,081
4	0,030	0,135	0,072	0,014	0,052	0,074
5	0,017	0,095	0,060	0,052	0,013	0,050
6	0,073	0,139	0,102	0,063	0,047	0,015

Table 6.
Total relation matrix for main risk criteria (T).

Criteria	"ri – cj"	"ri + cj"	Group definiton	Criteria	"ri – cj"	"ri + cj"	Group definiton
1	0,28	0,77	Cause	4	0,05	0,71	Cause
2	−0,30	1,01	Effect	5	0,04	0,54	Cause
3	−0,06	0,83	Effect	6	0,01	0,87	Cause

Table 7.
Cause and effect groups for main risk criteria.

Criteria below the threshold value were determined as affected (effect) criteria, and criteria above the threshold value were determined as affecting (cause) criteria [33].

Values below the threshold value of 0.07 for the main risk criterion total relationship matrix are shown with "-" and presented in **Table 8**. Similarly, threshold values were calculated for the sub-risk criteria groups.

According to the values in **Table 8**, a cause and effect diagram was produced for the main risk criterion matrix, which is shown in **Figure 2**. Similarly, cause and effect diagrams were produced for the sub-risk criteria groups.

T matrisi	1	2	3	4	5	6
1	—	0,16	0,126	—	—	0,115
2	—	—	0,073	0,071	—	0,092
3	—	0,112	—	—	—	0,081
4	—	0,135	0,072	—	—	0,074
5	—	0,095	—	—	—	—
6	0,073	0,139	0,102	—	—	—

Table 8.
Illustration of values above and below the threshold value.

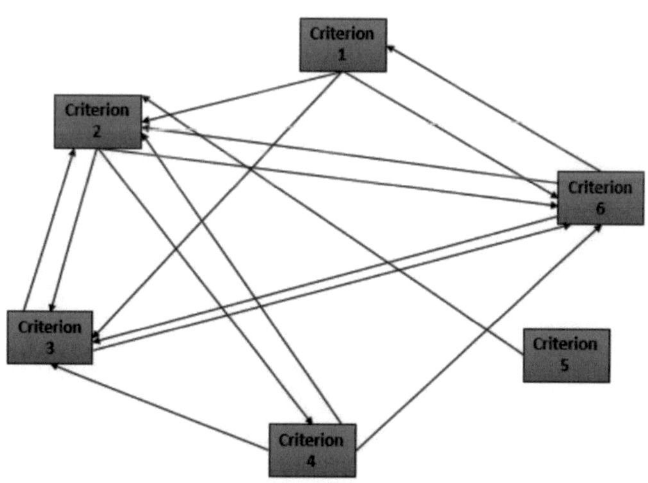

Figure 2.
Cause and effect diagram for the main risk criterion matrix.

Step 9: Calculation of criterion weights

Main risk criteria weights and sub-risk criteria weights were calculated using Eq. (13) and the results are presented in **Table 9**. The final weights were obtained by multiplying the weights of the main criteria and the weights of the sub-criteria. The final weights are shown in **Table 9**.

Step 10: Classification of criteria

Based on the criteria weights, the criteria were classified as high-, moderate-, and low-risk groups together with the expert group. While making this classification, risks with a value between 0 and 0.035 were included in the low-risk group, risks with a value between 0.035 and 0.045 were included in the moderate-risk group, and finally risks with a value above 0.045 were included in the high-risk group. The risk groups according to the weights of the criteria are shown in **Table 10**.

Main criteria	Main criterion weight	Sub criteria	Weights	Final weights
Human resources	0,17	1	0,10	0,018
		2	0,30	0,050
		3	0,32	0,054
		4	0,28	0,048
Assessment and certification activities	0,22	1	0,20	0,044
		2	0,19	0,041
		3	0,21	0,045
		4	0,21	0,046
		5	0,20	0,044
İnternal verification activities	0,17	1	0,23	0,038
		2	0,23	0,039
		3	0,22	0,037
		4	0,21	0,035
		5	0,17	0,029
Assessment material	0,15	1	0,26	0,039
		2	0,25	0,039
		3	0,21	0,039
		4	0,28	0,039
Physical and technical facilities	0,11	1	0,25	0,027
		2	0,24	0,027
		3	0,24	0,026
		4	0,27	0,029
Impartiality and reliability	0,18	1	0,24	0,043
		2	0,23	0,042
		3	0,23	0,042
		4	0,30	0,053

Table 9.
Table showing main criterion weights, sub-criteria weights, and final weights.

No	Sub criteria	Definition of risk criteria	Final weight	Risk group
1	A3	Assessors and internal verifiers do not have sufficient knowledge and experience.	0,054	High
2	F4	Failure to take adequate precautions for reliable assessment	0,053	High
3	A2	Failure of the assessor and internal verifiers to meet the assessor criteria	0,050	High
4	A4	Lack of awareness of the assessor and internal verifiers about the system	0,048	High
5	B4	Failure to perform assessment activities accurately, consistently, and reliably	0,046	High
6	B3	Assessor's failure to conduct exams in accordance with scenarios, checklists, and national qualifications	0,045	High
7	B1	The method used in theoretical and performance-based exams is not compatible with the qualifications.	0,044	Moderate
8	B5	Failure to make correct, consistent, fair, and reliable certification decisions	0,044	Moderate
9	F1	Lack of awareness of assessor and internal verifiers for consistent and fair assessment.	0,043	Moderate
10	F2	Possible conflicts of interest between assessors and candidates	0,042	Moderate
11	F3	The internal verifier has a conflict of interest with the candidate or assessor	0,042	Moderate
12	B2	Failure to conduct theoretical and performance-based exams in accordance with the guidelines	0,041	Moderate
13	D1	Not creating enough questions to meet the knowledge statements in the annex of the qualification units	0,039	Moderate
14	D2	The question booklets do not contain sufficient numbers and quality of questions to meet the knowledge statements.	0,039	Moderate
15	D3	Scenarios and checklists do not meet the skills and competencies in the annex of the qualification units	0,039	Moderate
16	D4	Failure to verify the suitability of materials used in assessment processes	0,039	Moderate
17	C2	Failure to perform internal verification activities in accordance with national qualifications	0,039	Moderate
18	C1	Failure to operate internal verification activity for each national qualification, qualification unit, and assessor	0,038	Moderate
19	C3	Failure of internal verifiers to make accurate, consistent, and fair assessments	0,037	Moderate
20	C4	Inadequate creation of the sampling plan in internal verification activities	0,035	Moderate
21	E4	Failure to take adequate measures to ensure the reliability of equipment	0,029	Low
22	C5	Failure to take corrective actions for detected nonconformities within the scope of internal verification	0,029	Low
23	E1	Inadequate physical environments to measure skills and competencies	0,027	Low

No	Sub criteria	Definition of risk criteria	Final weight	Risk group
24	E2	Failure to take adequate OHS measures in the areas where performance-based assessments are held	0,027	Low
25	E3	Equipment and materials are not suitable for measuring skills and competencies	0,026	Low
26	A1	Insufficient employment of assessors and internal verifiers	0,018	Low

Table 10.
Risk groups to which the criteria belong.

6. Development of a new risk management model

The weights of the risk criteria were calculated by the fuzzy DEMATEL method and classified as high, moderate, and low-risk groups according to the data obtained. The effects that the risks will create in case of occurrence are classified as shown in **Table 11**.

The "Risk Decision Matrix" in Appendix **Table A1** was created by utilizing the risk criterion weights and impact scores. It was obtained by dividing the weights of the risk criteria (importance of the risks) into the matrix depending on the effective value of the risks in case of occurrence.

The five-point value scale developed by Liberatore was used to rank the impact values of the risks. This scale consists of excellent, good, moderate, mediocre, and weak points [36]. This scale is adapted to classify effect values as very low, low, medium, high, and very high.

For example, the weight of the risk of "the assessor and internal verifiers do not have sufficient knowledge and experience" was determined as 0.054. The resulting weight was multiplied by "1000." The effects that the risk will create in case of occurrence and their scores are listed in the "Risk Decision Matrix" in Appendix **Table A1**. Accordingly, the score of the risk in case of very high impact is 0.054, in case of high impact "(4*0.054)/5", in case of medium impact "(3*0.054)/5", in case of low impact "(2*0.054)/5," and in case of very low impact, it was calculated as "(1*0.054)/5." Similar calculations were made for all sub-risk criteria.

The actions to be taken in case of occurrence of risks according to the risk decision matrix are shown in **Table 12**. The actions to be taken by Vocational Qualification Authority in case of occurrence of the risk are determined together with the expert group.

Impact level	Numerical value
Very low	1
Low	2
Moderate	3
High	4
Very high	5

Table 11.
The effects that the risk will create in case of occurrence.

Numerical value	Color of the region	Preventive actions to be taken by the organization depending on the risk value	Action to be taken by VQA in case of occurrence of risk
0–10	Light gray	Initiation of preventive action	Nonconformity to be corrected
11–20	Gray	Not taking assessment/postponing assessment before the preventive action is completed	Suspension of assesments
21–30	Blue	Not accepting the candidate application before the preventive action is completed	Cancelation of assesments
31–40	Light red	Not accepting the candidate application without internal verification and reverification of all processes and elements related to assessment activities	Suspension of authority
41 and above	Red		Withdrawal of authority

Table 12.
Precautions to be taken against risk and actions to be taken in case of occurrence.

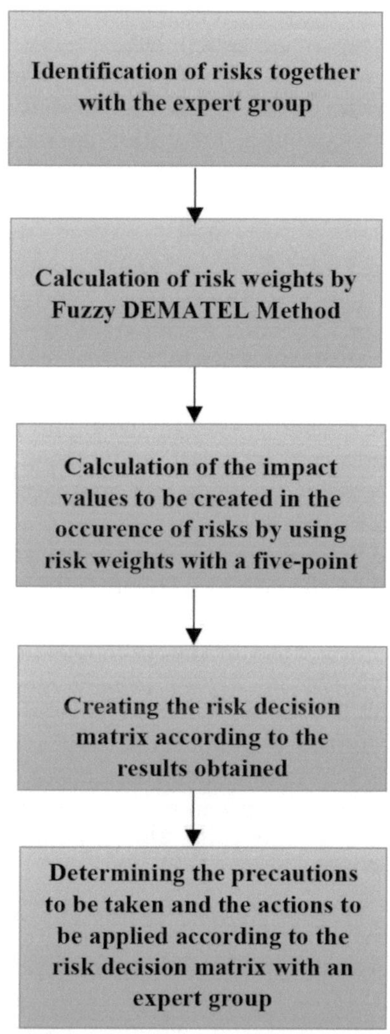

Figure 3.
The flow of the new risk management model.

As a result, a new risk management model has been proposed for organizations to evaluate risks related to measurement and evaluation activities and to take necessary precautions. The flow of the new risk management model is presented in **Figure 3**.

7. Conclusion

Risk management is defined as the activities aimed at identifying the risks that businesses may encounter and evaluating and reducing these risks. The subject of risk management is to define, evaluate, and respond appropriately to events or situations that are likely to occur and are considered to affect the achievement of the goals and objectives of the administration when they occur [15].

Thanks to risk management, businesses identify the risks involved in the activities they perform, evaluate the possibility of the risks to occur and the effect when they occur, plan the necessary preventive actions, and thus turn the threat or danger element posed by the risks into an advantage [12].

Within the scope of the study, the possible risks to be encountered in the assessment and certification activities of the certification bodies authorized by the Vocational Qualifications Authority, a public institution operating in Turkey, were evaluated. The possible risks in the assessment activities of the organizations were determined, and the fuzzy DEMATEL method, which is one of the Fuzzy Multi-Criteria Decision Making Methods, was used to evaluate the risks.

For the application of the method, a questionnaire questioning the effect status among the risk criteria was designed. The designed questionnaire was applied to a group of experts consisting of 12 people. At this stage, the CFCS (Converting Fuzzy Data into Crisp Scores) defuzzification method, which was developed by Opricovic and Tzeng (2003) for the application of fuzzy DEMATEL, was used [30, 31].

The answers given to the questionnaires by the expert group were converted into fuzzy numbers and these numbers were clarified by using the CFCS method. The relations and risk weights between the main risk groups, the relations between the sub-risks under the main risk groups, and the sub-risk weights were determined. The final weights were obtained by integrating the main risk criteria weights and sub-risk criteria weights. Depending on the criterion weights, the risks are classified as low, moderate, and high.

As a result of the calculations made within the scope of fuzzy DEMATEL, it was determined that the criterion with the highest priority among the main risk criteria groups was "Assessment and Certification Activities" with a score of 0.22. This criterion was followed by "Impartiality and Reliability" with 0.18 points, "Internal Verification Activities" with 0.17 and "Human Resources" with 0.17 points. While the main criteria of internal verification and human resources were of equal importance, "Assessment Material" with 0.15 points and "Physical and Technical Facilities" with 0.11 points followed these criteria.

When the sub-risk criteria are examined within the scope of the main criteria, it has been determined that the criteria with the highest priority and accordingly the high-risk group are generally sub-criteria within the scope of the human resources main criterion.

It was determined that the criteria defined under assessment and certification activities came in second place, and the criteria within the scope of impartiality and reliability took the third place. While the criteria for impartiality and reliability, assessment material, and internal verification are generally in the moderate-risk group, the criteria for physical and technical facilities are in the low-risk group.

It has been observed that the distribution of the criteria to risk groups (low, moderate, and high) is homogeneous. Validity and reliability of assessment and certification activities depend on the competence of the assessors and internal verifiers, and the risks that may arise from the assessors and internal verifiers pose a high risk in terms of the validity and reliability of the related activities. For this reason, the fact that the sub-risk criteria weights due to human resources are high and they are included in the high-risk group have been evaluated as a suitable result by the expert group.

The weights of the risks have been determined, the effects to be created in the assessment and certification activities in case of occurrence of the risks have been calculated, and the activities to be carried out according to the obtained results have been determined. The effects of the risks in case of occurrence are classified as very low, low, moderate, high, and very high. Impact values were assigned as one for very low, two for low, three for moderate, four for high, and five for very high.

By making use of the five-point value scale, the risk criteria weights were distributed to the matrix depending on the impact value of the risks in case of occurrence, and the "Risk Decision Matrix" was obtained. In line with the results obtained from the matrix, the precautions that should be applied by the institutions and the sanctions to be applied in case the risks occur in the systems of the institutions were determined.

As a result, a new risk management model was designed for the assessment and management of risks. The new model designed both offers a new approach and guides the institutions in the management of the risks in the assessment activities of the assessment and certification bodies. It is evaluated that the stages defined in the new risk management model designed can be used in many different fields of activity, and thus, businesses operating in various sectors and fields can identify and measure the possible risks in their system. According to risk value obtained by using this model, they can determine the necessary precautions and sanctions.

Thanks

The author of the chapter would like to thank Prof. Dr. Abdullah Süreyya ERSOY and also the managers and employees of the Vocational Qualifications Authority who supported the necessary work for the writing of the chapter.

A. Appendix

Weights				Impact value				
Group of risks	**Number of sub-criteria**	**Final weights**	**Final weights *1000**	**Very low (1)**	**Low (2)**	**Moderate (3)**	**High (4)**	**Very high (5)**
High	A3	0,054	54	11	22	32	43	54
High	F4	0,053	53	11	21	32	42	53
High	A2	0,050	50	10	20	30	40	50
High	A4	0,048	48	10	19	29	38	48
High	B4	0,046	46	9	18	28	37	46
High	B3	0,045	45	9	18	27	36	45
Moderate	B1	0,044	44	9	18	26	35	44
Moderate	B5	0,044	44	9	18	26	35	44
Moderate	F1	0,043	43	9	17	26	34	43
Moderate	F2	0,042	42	8	17	25	34	42
Moderate	F3	0,042	42	8	17	25	34	42
Moderate	B2	0,041	41	8	16	25	33	41
Moderate	D1	0,039	39	8	16	23	31	39
Moderate	D2	0,039	39	8	16	23	31	39
Moderate	D3	0,039	39	8	16	23	31	39
Moderate	D4	0,039	39	8	16	23	31	39
Moderate	C2	0,039	39	8	16	23	31	39
Moderate	C1	0,038	38	8	15	23	30	38
Moderate	C3	0,037	37	7	15	22	30	37
Moderate	C4	0,035	35	7	14	21	28	35
Low	E4	0,029	29	6	12	17	23	29
Low	C5	0,029	29	6	12	17	23	29
Low	E1	0,027	27	5	11	16	22	27
Low	E2	0,027	27	5	11	16	22	27
Low	E3	0,026	26	5	10	16	21	26
Low	A1	0,018	18	4	7	11	14	18

Table A1.
Risk decision matrix.

Author details

Yaprak Akçay Zileli
Vocational Qualifications Authority (VQA), Ankara, Turkey

*Address all correspondence to: yaprakzileli@gmail.com

References

[1] Kızıldağ D. Yönetsel Açıdan Risk Yönetimine Bir Bakış: ISO 31000 Risk Yönetimi. 1st ed. Vol. 43. Ankara: Seçkin Yayıncılık; 2011. p. 47

[2] Regulation of the Duties, Authorities and Responsibilities of the Vocational Qualifications Authority operating in Turkey: Article 237 of the Presidential Decree No. 4 [Internet]. 2018. Available from: https://www.myk.gov.tr/images/articles/Mevzuat/19.5.4_v2.pdf [Accessed November 25, 2022]

[3] Authorization Criteria and Implementation Guide for Vocational Qualifications Authority Certification Bodies [Internet]. 2018. Available from: https://www.myk.gov.tr/images/articles/denetim/SBD.RHB.004Belgelendirme_Kuruluslari_icin_Yetkilendirme_Kriterleri_ve_Uygulama_Rehberi_Rev.00.pdf [Accessed: November 25, 2022]

[4] Akçay G. Kurumsal Risk Yönetiminde İç Denetimin Rolü ve Kamu İdarelerinde Yaşanan Gelişmeler. Denetişim Dergisi. 2011;7:25-46. Available from: https://dergipark.org.tr/tr/pub/denetisim/issue/22497/240537. [Accessed: November 25, 2022]

[5] Usman Ö. Preparation of risk assessment reports In Enterprise risk management system. OPUS–International Journal of Society Researches. 2018;**9**(16):1586-1612. DOI: 10.26466/opus.479277

[6] Chapman RJ. Simple Tools and Techniques for Enterprise Risk Management. 1st ed. Wet Sussex: John Wiley and Sons; 2006

[7] Akçay ZY. Development of a Risk Management Model Using Fuzzy Multi-Criteria Decision Making Method. Ankara: Gazi University Institute of Social Sciences; 2019

[8] Gacar A. Early identification of risks and risk management committees In the context of Enterprise risk management In businesses: A qualitative research In Istanbul stock exchange. Dumlupınar University Journal of Social Sciences. 2017;**52**:123-133

[9] Morgan S. Clinical Risk Management: A Clinical Tool and Practitioner's Manual. London: Sainsbury Centre for Mental Health; 2000

[10] Özkilic Ö. Hazard and Risk Concepts – Terminology. In: 5th International Conference on Occupational Health and Safety. Istanbul; 2008

[11] Turkish Standards Institution. TS ISO 31000: 2011 Risk Management-Principles and Guidelines. Ankara: Turkish Standards Institution Publication; 2011. p. 5

[12] Küçükoğlu M. Where we are in risk management? Example of automotive industry. Trakya University Journal of Social Science. 2020;**22**(2):1001-1020. DOI: 10.26468/trakyasobed.567567

[13] Enterprise Risk Management Integrating with Strategy and Performance [Internet]. 2017. Available from: https://www.coso.org/Shared%20Documents/2017-COSO-ERM-Integrating-with-Strategy-and-Performance-Executive-Summary.pdf [Accessed: November 30, 2022]

[14] International Organization for Standardization. ISO 31000:2018 Risk Management-Guidelines. Geneva: International Organization for Standardization; 2018

[15] Public Internal Control Guide. 2014. Available from: https://ms.hmb.gov.tr/uploads/2019/08/8227kamuic

kontrolrehberi1versiyon12.pdf [Accessed: November 30, 2022]

[16] Anderson EJ. Business Risk Management: Models and Analysis. 1st ed. United States: John Wiley and Sons; 2013

[17] Regulation About the Preparation of National Occupational Standards and National Qualifications [Internet]. 2015. Available from: https://www.myk.gov.tr/index.php/tr/mevzuat [Accessed: November 30, 2022]

[18] Regulation About the Vocational Qualifications Authority Examination, Assessment, Evaluation and Certification [Internet]. 2015. Available from: https://www.myk.gov.tr/index.php/tr/mevzuat [Accessed: November 30, 2022]

[19] Gabus A, Fontela E. Perceptions of the World Problematique: Communication Procedure, Communicating with Those Bearing Collective Responsibility. Geneva: Battelle Geneva Research Centre; 1973

[20] Chen C. A FuzzyApproach to select the location of the distribution Center. Fuzzy Sets and Systems. 2011;**118**(1): 65-73. DOI: 10.1016/S0165-0114(98)00459-X

[21] Korucu AT. Design of a Turkish Visual Interface for Fuzzy Logic Problems [Thesis]. Konya: Selcuk University Institute of Science; 2007

[22] Lin C, Wu W. A causal analytical method for group decision-making under fuzzy environment. Expert Systems with Applications. 2008;**34**(1): 205-213. DOI: 10.1016/j.eswa.2006.08.012

[23] Zargar SM, Javidnia M, Shahhosseini M. Using Fuzzy DEMATEL method for analyzing the Technology Acceptance Model 2: A case study. In: 3rd International Conference on Advanced Management Science. Malaysia; 2011. pp. 88-93

[24] Chang YY, Kuan MJ, Chuang YC, Tzeng GH. Exploring the SPM system structure model by using fuzzy DEMATEL for NPD. In: Fuzzy Systems International Conference. Taipe, Taiwan: IEEE; 2011b. pp. 1491-1496

[25] Ying-Chyi C, Chia-Chi S, Hsin-Yi Y. Evaluating the criteria for human resource for science and technology (HRST) based on an integrated fuzzy AHP and fuzzy DEMATEL approach. Applied Soft Computing. 2012;**12**(1): 64-71. DOI: 10.1016/j.asoc.2011.08.058

[26] Akyuz E, Çelik E. A fuzzy DEMATEL method to evaluate critical operational hazards during gas freeing process in crude oil tanks. Journal of Loss Prevention in the Process Industries. 2015;**38**:243-453. DOI: 10.1016/j.jlp.2015.10.006

[27] Seker S, Zavadskas EK. Application of fuzzy DEMATEL method for analyzing occupational risks on construction sites. Sustainability. 2017; **9**(11):2083. DOI: 10.3390/su9112083

[28] Mahmoudi S, Jalali A, Ahmadi M, Abasi P, Salari N. Identifying critical success factors in heart failure self-care using fuzzy DEMATEL method. Applied Soft Computing. 2019;**84**:105729. DOI: 10.1016/j.asoc.2019.105729

[29] Feng C, Ma R. Identification of the factors that influence service innovation in manufacturing enterprises by using the fuzzy DEMATEL method. Journal of Cleaner Production. 2020;**253**:120002. DOI: 10.1016/j.jclepro.2020.120002

[30] Opricovic S, Tzeng GH. Defuzzification within a multicriteria

decision model. International Journal of Uncertainty, Fuzziness and Knowledge-Based Systems. 2003;**11**(5):635-652. DOI: 10.1142/S0218488503002387

[31] Zhou Q, Huang W, Zhang Y. Identifying critical success factors in emergency management using a fuzzy DEMATEL method. Safety Science. 2011;**49**(2):243-252. DOI: 10.1016/j.ssci.2010.08.005

[32] Şenocak AA. An Application of Sustainable Supplier Selection Problem Based on Multi Criteria Decision Making and Linear Programming in Fuzzy Environment. Denizli: Pamukkale Unıversity Institute of Science; 2016

[33] Kaushik S, Somvir R. DEMATEL: A methodology for research in library and information science. International Journal of Librarianship and Administration. 2015;**6**(2):179-185

[34] Dalalah D, Hayajneh M, Batieha F. A fuzzy multi-criteria decision making model for supplier selection. Expert Systems with Applications. 2011;**38**(7):8384-8391. DOI: 10.1016/j.eswa.2011.01.031

[35] Wang YL, Tzeng GH. Brand Marketing for creating brand value based on a MCDM model combining DEMATEL with ANP and VIKOR methods. Experts Systems with Applications. 2012;**39**(5):5600-5615. DOI: 10.1016/j.eswa.2011.11.057

[36] Liberatore MJ, Nydick RL, Sanchez PM. The evaluation of research papers. Interfaces. 1992;**22**(2):92-100. DOI: 10.1287/inte.22.2.92

Section 2

Sustainability

Chapter 3

Climate and Environmental Risk Action: A Call for Fresh Commitments to Adaptation and Resilience in West African Sub-Region

Bolaji Abdulkadir Usman

Abstract

Problem of capacity to adapt and build resilience against climate and environmental risks has become a major source of concern globally. However, poorer regions and countries where substantial proportions of the people depend more on natural capital are generally more at risk. West Africa is a region known to have experienced major environmental changes in the last half century. Therefore, using evidences from the literature, this chapter examines climate and other environmental problems that have created challenges to agriculture and food security, water resources, health, energy and infrastructural development. We highlight the potential for adaptation and building resilience, while also emphasising the need to develop appropriate adaptation and risk management strategies built on proper understanding of dimensions of exposure and vulnerability. Among other recommendations, this chapter accentuates the need for raising climate and environmental risk awareness among the populace, sustainable management and use of natural resources, development of weather information and early warning systems and stronger transnational cooperation to address climate and other environmental risk impacts.

Keywords: climate, environmental risk, adaptation, resilience, risk impact

1. Introduction

Climate change has emerged as one of the most prominent environmental, economic and social threats facing humanity today. Climate and environmental risks are associated with extreme weather events like drought, flooding, windstorm, rise in sea levels, earthquakes and volcanic eruptions that may result in ecosystem degradation, loss of natural assets, potential trade and supply chain disruptions, reduced productivity, declining welfare and loss of lives and properties. Consequently, across the globe the probable impacts of extreme weather events and other environmental hazards and the problem of capacity to adapt and build resilience against the impacts, have become a source of great concern. While international organizations, governments, non-governmental organizations (NGOs) and corporations are responding by building environmental factors into economic, social and political structures to strengthen resilience and adapt to changing conditions, these challenges are proving difficult to manage. It has thus been argued that addressing these challenges require introduction of appropriate incentives, taking efficient economic decisions and promoting changes in households and public institutions in order to change habits and behave in an environmentally friendly way [1, 2].

The global socio-economic impacts of climate change are expected to become more substantial as affected regions continue to grow in number and size, and more people and more natural capital would be negatively affected in the near future. Although, all countries of the world are affected by climate change, poorer regions and countries are generally more at risk as their populations often rely more on natural capital and have less financial resources to adapt quickly [3]. Africa is highly exposed to climate and other environmental risks because it has experienced warming trends of between 0.26°C and 0.5°C per decade in the last one century [4]. It is believed that this trend will continue and may significantly increase with much negative implications in the form of considerable increase in temperature, decreasing rainfall and increasing frequency and intensity of tropical storms. The continent is known to contain about half of the world's most risk prone countries and it is experiencing increasing number of disasters. The number of reported disasters resulting from natural hazards has particularly increased on the continent over the last three decades, with floods, epidemics and drought being most prominent [5]. Climate change, poor urban planning, environmental degradation and fragility, poverty, inequality and conflicts have been found to be the main disaster drivers on the continent. The impact on the human population are in form of increase in exposure to water stress, decline in production of staple food crops and increase in poverty and conflicts due to loss of livelihoods [1, 5, 6].

As a result of increasing climatic variability and human activities, West Africa and particularly the Sahel region, has experienced major environmental changes within the last half century. The Sahel is regarded as the region that experienced the greatest rainfall anomalies in the world during the last century [7]. Observations have shown general warming across West Africa since the 1960s, increase in incidence of warm spells and decrease in incidence of cold days. Overall decrease in annual rainfall has also been observed since the 1960s, while the arid zones have experienced more prolonged droughts since the 1970s [7, 8] Although, projected climatic models for West Africa differ based on the assumptions, most agree on overall warming trend across the region, with average temperature rise of 0.5% per decade. There is also general consensus on an overall decline in precipitation across the region of 0.5–40% by 2025, and average sea level rise of 0.5–1.0 m by 2100 [8].

Devastating droughts, changes in seasons, reduced and unpredictable rainfall and flash floods have negatively affected local community livelihoods and resulted in population displacements. As a result of these climatic and humanitarian crises, West Africa is now viewed as a region of poverty, conflict and human insecurity [9]. Many parts of West Africa face chronic variability of rainfall and strong pressure on arable land. The situation is made more critical by the fact that agriculture and livestock which depend heavily on the ecosystem creates about 60% of household incomes. Furthermore, due to increasing population the people are forced to adopt unsustainable practices in order to survive. This makes the environment more vulnerable to degradation and increase in fragility of marginal areas [9]. This paper was conceived to explore climate and environmental risks and the potential for raising adaptive capacity and resilience in West Africa. Against this backdrop the specific objectives are to: investigate the climate and environmental risks; examine the dimensions of vulnerabilities and impacts; determine the adaptation and resilience opportunities; and propose policy options to be adopted to raise adaptive capacity and resilience in the sub-region.

The remaining part of this paper is subdivided into five sections. The section succeeding this introduction focuses on definition and clarification of major concepts relevant to this paper. The next section highlights the main climate and environmental risks in West Africa, while also emphasising the vulnerability of the human population. Using evidences from literature, the succeeding section presents climate and environmental risk impacts and potential for action in major sectors. The next section outlines strategies that can be targeted towards raising adaptive capacity and resilience in West Africa. The concluding section summarizes the key findings and suggests areas for future research.

2. Conceptual clarifications

2.1 Risk

Risk is the combination of the likelihood or probability of an event and its consequences. However, risk could be defined from either the natural hazard based approach or the vulnerability based approach. In the hazard based approach the likelihood is seen in relation to the hazard, in which situation risk is seen as the likelihood of a hazard and its consequences. This is also called event risk. Alternatively, using the vulnerability based approach; the likelihood is attached to the consequences whereby risk is the likelihood of exceeding a given level of damage, otherwise known as outcome risk [10, 11]. Nevertheless, in both cases risk is explicitly or implicitly associated with a "trigger" event or hazard and impacts defined by the characteristics of the exposed system [11]. Risk does not only depend on climate and other environmental events (hazards) but is also determined by exposure and vulnerability to the hazard [12]. Hazard is broadly defined as a process or occurrence of natural origin or due to human action with potential to cause injury, loss of life or other health impacts, damage to property, disruption of social and economic wellbeing or degradation of the environment [10, 13]. Natural hazards are mostly associated with potentially destructive natural processes and phenomena like earthquakes, floods or windstorms and so on [14].

2.2 Vulnerability

Vulnerability is generally defined as the likelihood that a person or group of people will be exposed to and adversely affected by a hazard [15]. As it relates to climate change, vulnerability is defined as the degree of susceptibility of a system to the adverse effect of climate variability and extremes. It is the likelihood that assets (people, buildings, farmlands and so on) would be destroyed or damaged when exposed to hazard [14]. Vulnerability is a function of three constituents which are exposure, sensitivity and adaptive capacity [16, 17], which are important for establishing the level of vulnerability of a system to climate change and also provide necessary information for evaluating and reducing climate threats [18, 19].

Exposure is described as the inventory of elements or location, attributes and value of assets that could be affected in an area in which hazard events may occur [12, 13]. Therefore, if people and economic assets are not situated in (exposed to) potentially perilous situation, issue of disaster risk will not exist. Hence, while it is possible to be exposed but not vulnerable (if there is enough means to modify the environment and behaviour to mitigate potential loss), vulnerability to extreme event requires exposure [12]. Sensitivity refers to the degree (extent) to which people, property and other assets could be harmed by exposure to hazard. In other words it indicates the potential for adverse impacts [20]. Indicators of exposure include increasing temperature, windstorms, sea level rise and drought, while sensitivity to hazard depends on geographic and socio-economic conditions like natural environmental condition, demographic conditions and level of dependency on natural assets [19].

Adaptive capacity refers to the ability of individuals, group or system to adjust to environmental changes, moderate potential damages, take advantage of opportunities or cope with consequences of event like climatic extremes [21, 22]. In other words, it is the responsiveness to stress in living conditions or shocks associated with extreme conditions. Adaptive capacity encompasses the social and technical skills and strategies of individuals or groups directed towards responding to environmental (or social and economic) changes [22]. For instance, highly managed agricultural and water resources systems in developed countries are expected to be more adaptable than those that are less managed. Adaptive capacity may also be exemplified by ability to shift to alternate land use within an agro system or ability to adopt drought resistant crops [21, 22].

2.3 Adaptation

Adaptation is simply any human action which minimizes the adverse effect of climate change while maximizing its advantages. It is the adjustment carried out in response to actual or expected climatic or other environmental stimuli, which moderates or takes advantage of beneficial opportunities. Adaptation therefore involves changes in attitudes, practices and institutions to reduce or offset probable damages or take advantage of opportunities associated with climate change [21, 23, 24].

The ability of a system to adapt depends on some characteristics of the system consisting of sensitivity, vulnerability, resilience and adaptive capacity, also referred to as the "determinants of adaption" [18, 23]. Adaptation has been classified into different forms. Adaptation could be autonomous or spontaneous, planned, passive, anticipatory or reactive. In addition, adaptation can be short or long term, localized or widespread. Spontaneous adaptations are reactive in nature because they emanate after initial impact has manifested (normally without the intervention of a public agency). Planned adaptation may be anticipatory (when carried out before impacts have manifested) or may also be reactive [18, 24].

2.4 Resilience

Resilience is the degree of shock or change that a system can withstand while still maintaining its structure, basic operations and organizations. It thus describes the ability of a system (or community) to endure and utilize or even benefit from adversities, shocks or stresses, in both short and long terms. This implies that resilient systems may even benefit from adversities, if they are strong enough [22, 25]. Therefore, a resilient system is expected to possess the ability to anticipate and respond to perilous events, trends or disruptions related to climate or other environmental risks.

At both individual and community levels resilience is usually greater when there is higher level of social infrastructure that facilitates sharing of knowledge and resources in response to shocks and disruption associated with climate and environmental threats. Social safety nets such as mutual assistance within families and communities strengthen people's resilience. In addition, social learning is a major way through which people learn new techniques depending on the prevalent situation in an area [22].

3. Climate and environmental risks in West Africa

Climate change has become a major global challenge, but some geographical regions of the world are more affected than others. Due to socio-economic circumstances and meteorological conditions, African countries are particularly vulnerable to climate and environmental risks. In West Africa, increasing climate variability and human activities has resulted in major environmental changes. Rising temperatures, increasing erratic rainfall pattern and more frequent droughts, degradation and desertification of productive lands, flooding and inundation of coastal areas due to increasing sea level are some of the major environmental problems in the sub-region. These have created challenges to food security and management of land, water and other resources. Most significant is that the last five decades have witnessed recurrent drought episodes that have resulted in serious degradation of natural capital and ecosystems and recurrent food crises within the sub-region [10, 26, 27]. These problems are exacerbated by the rapidly increasing human population. For instance, the human population of West Africa was estimated to be 397 million in 2018 with an annual growth rate of 2.4% since 1980 [10].

These challenges are particularly dire for rural communities in the sub-region, where crop cultivation, livestock rearing and fishery which are highly dependent on climate, are the main sources of livelihood. Rural environmental degradation and increasing population and poverty are escalating the stress on environmental resources and has become a major driver of rural-urban population drift. The rate of urbanization in West Africa is over 4% per year, with 43% of the population living in cities, and this is projected to increase to 63% by the year 2050 [10, 26]. The combined effects of high level of poverty and high reliance on rain-fed agriculture and poor access to resources and services have resulted in high vulnerability to climate and environmental risks in the sub-region. Various studies [26, 28–30] have found that poverty, low level of technology, poor access to health care services and general infrastructural deficiencies among other factors are closely linked to disaster vulnerability in West African countries, and that repeated exposure to stress further exacerbates poverty in the region. Environmental degradation is a major contributing factor for conflict and food insecurity. Degradation or depletion of natural resources and population pressure are known to trigger competition for scarce resources such as arable land and water, which often results in tension and conflict [28].

4. Climate and environmental risk impact and potential for action in key sectors

4.1 Agriculture and food security

4.1.1 Vulnerabilities and impacts

Farming and other rural livelihood activities in West Africa are highly vulnerable to the impacts of climate change. For instance, drought, floods, windstorms and epidemics have been identified as the main climate and environmental risks the people are exposed to in Burkina Faso, Niger, Ghana, Nigeria and Benin [26, 28–30]. Drought often causes widespread crop failures, particularly where rain-fed agriculture is the dominant farming practice. Furthermore, successive floods and drought greatly reduce the ability to store food for future use, with great negative impacts on food security [29]. Decrease in land productivity and crop yields has become a threat to the survival of large number of people and livelihoods in in the region. The environmental stressors like drought have combined with anthropogenic factors like destruction of forest cover and increasing use of intensive cultivation to result in decline in soil fertility and associated decline in ecological resilience [31].

For example, food insecurity was reported to be very high in northern Ghana, as 60% of the rural households have insufficient food during four months of the year. Furthermore, as a result of unpredictability of rainfall many farmers have experienced significant decrease in yields, and often find it difficult to know when to plant [26]. In Burkina Faso where agriculture employs almost 90% of the active population smallholder rain-fed agriculture is the mainstay of the economy, the country is also characterizes by chronic food insecurity with many households finding it difficult to satisfy their food needs [28, 29]. Similarly, in Niger the trend of increasing temperatures, decreasing rainfall coupled with increasing land degradation has emerged as the main challenge to agricultural productivity and food security. In addition, increasing population pressure has pushed agricultural expansion into marginal lands, further increasing environmental degradation [29, 32].

Most other countries in the sub-region also face similar situations. For example, Togo which has about 70% of the working population in agriculture is also highly vulnerable to natural disasters in the form of drought, flooding and windstorms. The country experienced three major droughts and eight major riverine flooding events from 1900 to 2020, with a combined total of over one million people affected

Natural hazard	Subtype	Event count	Total deaths	Total affected	Total damage ('000 USD)
Drought	Drought	10	0	550,000	500
Epidemic	Bacterial disease	3	1032	11,610	0
	Viral disease	2	84	560	0
Flood		8	72	547,695	0
Storm		1	0	15	200

Source: World Bank [30].

Table 1.
Natural disasters in Togo, 1900–2020.

DOI: http://dx.doi.org/10.5772/intechopen.106428

(**Table 1**). It is projected that increasing temperatures would affect productivity of key crops like coffee, cocoa and maize and also increase the prevalence of pest and diseases in the country. The last four decades in particular have witnessed many floods that have devastated large areas of cultivated lands [30].

4.1.2 Adaptation and resilience options

Some adaptation options for crop production include adoption and promotion of conservation agriculture, agroforestry, water management, cultivar development, fertilizer efficiency, changes in planting dates, restoration of degraded lands and seasonal weather and climate services [10, 33–36]. For instance, agroforestry (integrating trees with crops) has many advantages if carried out correctly. The trees serve as 'nutrient pumps' by helping to bring nutrients that are too deep for crops, while their leaves also serve as mulch that might suppress some weed growth and also protect the soil from intense heat. In addition, the litter will be transformed to organic matter while the trees also contribute to adaptation by helping to screen the crops from strong winds [35].

There is also a lot of potential for improving water management in form of irrigation and water harvesting. For instance, it has been estimated that out of the 75.5 million hectares of arable land available in the region, only 1.2% (917,000 ha) benefit from irrigation, while only 0.8% (635,000 ha) could be said to be under effective use [10]. However, it has been argued that it may be more beneficial to focus more on small scale private irrigation as against large scale public irrigation. This will ensure more efficient management and distribution of water [35, 36]. For example, farmer-managed irrigation in Mali and valley bottom irrigation in northern Nigeria and Niger have been found to very successful [37]. Great potential also exist for integrating aquaculture into irrigated plots so as to increase food production in the sub-region. For instance, many West African countries including Nigeria, Mali and Senegal among others have the essential resources required to produce large quantities of fish in irrigation schemes. In particular, rice-fish farming can be successfully adopted and implemented in many areas of West Africa [38–40]. There are also opportunities for the development and adoption of new varieties of cultivars. Introduction of varieties of cultivars that can withstand higher temperatures and varieties that are resilient to drought, pest, weeds, flooding and salinity will go a long way in ensuring higher adaptation and resilience to climate hazards.

Adoption of integrated soil fertility management, changing of planting dates and provision of seasonal weather and climates services are also important adaptation options. For instance, ensuring the application of the right type and quantity of fertilizer at the right time will guarantee efficient use by crops while minimizing emissions. Promotion of integrated soil fertility management will also ensure enhancement of soil organic matter and improve nutrient efficiency [35]. For example, adaptation options like late sowing, fertilizer use and increased planting density have been suggested for sorghum while promising effect of rainfall harvesting technique has been found in maize cultivation in West Africa [36]. Provision of weather and climate information services will raise adaptive capacity by helping farmers to plan their planting and make projection about rainfall distribution patterns and temperature variation. For instance, evidences from Ghana and Senegal have shown the importance of providing reliable information on weather and climate-smart agricultural practices through radio and mobile phone services to farmers [35].

4.2 Water resources

4.2.1 Vulnerabilities and impacts

Climate change, population pressure and economic development are posing major challenges to water resources management in West African countries. Inadequate access to water supply and frequent droughts and floods disrupts the livelihoods of the people. Flooding results in siltation and sedimentation of rivers and lakes, and pollution of surface waters. It may also create ecological condition for invasive species that may further change ecosystem structure and function. For instance, disruption of ecosystem structure may alter biological cycle of fish production in an area [41].

Droughts are associated with drying wells, fall in water body levels, rise in pollutant loads and general aggravation of water stress [29]. In the last five decades, West African rivers have experienced overall decline in water supply and it has been projected that river flows will decline by 20–40% by 2050 [29]. Reduced river flows are expected to encourage the spread of toxic water plants such as hyacinth. When this is combined with rising temperatures, it will cause further decline in water quality and encourage the spread of water borne diseases like malaria. Increased water stress will also aggravate other health conditions. For instance, diarrhoea is a major cause of childhood mortality in West Africa [30].

In addition, increase in water stress implies that people, particularly women and children would have to travel farther to access water for domestic uses, reducing their ability to engage in economic activities [29]. Already, three West African countries namely, Nigeria, Niger and Burkina Faso already belong to the group of 37 "hotspot" countries with largest number of children living in areas of high or extremely high water vulnerability [42]. Poor access to water normally increases vulnerability, considering the fact that access to water is essential for maintaining good health and the ability to cope with other stresses [31].

Along the coastal areas, rising sea levels and increasing sea surges will worsen the problems of salt water intrusion into inland freshwater bodies and may cause lakes and lagoons to become completely brackish, with serious negative implications on biodiversity, including mangrove population [29]. The importance of mangrove is such that it is known to buffer river basins and also protects water birds and river fish stock against ocean waves and saltwater invasion [41, 43]. For instance, in the

Countries	Submerged surface area (sq. km)	Surface area lost through erosion (sq. km)	Value of property affected (millions of USD)
Senegal	1650	28–44	355–464
The Gambia	46	—	—
Cote de Ivory	471	—	4710
Benin	17.5	22.5	—
Nigeria	8864	78–145	9003

Source: USAID [41].

Table 2.
Projected general impact of sea level rise by 2100 for selected West African countries.

Niger Delta sea surges and flooding pollutes water aquifers and rivers with sediment [44], with great negative implications on human health and human livelihood. Furthermore, salt intrusion on arable land in coastal areas may lead to loss of productive land. It has also been associated with crop substitution and dependence on one crop as an adaptation measure as observed in Guinea Bissau, which created further food insecurity and made the people more vulnerable to price fluctuations [45]. Many West African countries are vulnerable to the risk posed by sea level rise. **Table 2** show the general impact of projected sea level rise by 2100 for some West African Countries.

Additionally, increase in water shortages will fuel conflicts among communities depending on shared water bodies. Conflict over water resources is already becoming a problem in many areas within the sub-region. For instance, the shrinking of Lake Chad by about 90% is viewed as a major factor in the persistent conflict and violent extremism in the area [46]. The lake is very vital to the economy of the area as the primary supplier of fresh water for bordering communities in Nigeria, Niger, Cameroon and Chad. Climate change has led to increasing competition for land resources in the area resulting in conflicts among communities. The persistent insurgency in area has been linked to failed harvests, loss of livelihood, food insecurity, forced migration and poverty brought about by increasing water stress in the area [7, 46].

4.2.2 Adaptation and resilience options

Human activities and their impacts on water scarcity must be fully considered in drought risk management and policy. For instance, while land degradation reduces soil water holding capacity and increases vulnerability to drought, rehabilitation of degraded lands and enhancement of soil health are known to help create better resilience to drought [37]. Water conservation and supplementation in dry areas, adoption of integrated water storage and small reservoir systems have been successfully implemented in Mali, Ghana and Burkina Faso to improve water supply for agriculture [35]. Furthermore, reforestation schemes in the savannah regions of West Africa have shown evidence of increased river flow and ground water recharge [31].

However, adoption and implementation of integrated water resources management is very vital in adaptation to climate change. This will enable the integration of all aspects of the water system (surface water, underground water, water quality and so on) with all water related sectors (flood control, irrigation, water supply, industrial water and so on) and water use and control practices, to secure quantity and quality of water required for modern society [47]. The success of this approach requires the collection and sharing of relevant water data on quantity of water resources and water allocation (water demand, water intake, seasonal water changes and so on). The implementation involves efficient use of water resources to reduce vulnerability to climate change impacts such as adoption of crops with low water requirements, promotion of water saving irrigation technology (such as drip irrigation), reducing water use and raising public awareness. It also involves promoting groundwater recharge, controlling exploitation, monitoring groundwater levels, conserving groundwater quality, enhancing other sources of water supply (like rainwater harvesting and waste water treatment) and promoting water storage by boosting capacity of water resources development facilities [47, 48].

4.3 Human health

4.3.1 Vulnerabilities and impacts

West African countries are characterised by inadequate health infrastructure, services and access to health care, which make public health highly vulnerable to adverse effect of climate change [9]. Many adverse implications are attributable to projected temperature increase, decreasing rainfall, increased frequency and intensity of tropical rainstorms and increased duration and severity of aridity and drought. Expected health implications will be linked to increased water stress, rise in food shortages, and increased exposure and proliferation of infectious and vector borne diseases and heat related diseases [30]. Temperature and rainfall trends are expected to result in shift in the distribution, timing and severity of climate sensitive diseases like malaria and meningitis [49]. Heat stress and other related risks associated with cardiovascular and respiratory diseases are also expected to be on the rise due to increased heat waves, with children and the elderly in particular more likely to be impacted. Evidences already exist related to rising mortality associated with increasing heat in countries like Burkina Faso and Ghana. Deterioration of air quality due to dust is will also worsen the problem of cardiovascular and respiratory diseases in the region, considering the fact that increase in dust during the harmattan has been observed in countries like Nigeria and Togo [30, 49]. For example, in Nigeria 50% of the deaths related to ischaemic heart diseases, stroke, lung cancer and chronic obstructive pulmonary diseases among adults, and acute lower respiratory infections in children below 5 years in 2012, were attributable to household air infection [50].

Increasing water scarcity will worsen the intensity and spread of waterborne and water wash diseases as people are forced to depend more on unsafe sources of water in the drier areas. Poor water quality is a major threat to human health in West Africa. For example, it has been observed that 34% of the population in the sub-region lack access to safe drinking water, while 73% lack access to basic sanitation [42, 49]. In addition, there is high possibility that the rate and distribution of vector and waterborne diseases will be worsened by the warming temperatures, more frequent intense tropical storms and flooding. Nigeria faces great inland flood risk and it is projected that by 2030 an additional 801,700 people may be at risk of river floods annually due to climate change [50]. For instance, recurrence of cholera and diarrheal diseases are closely linked to heavy rains and flooding which bring contaminated water and sewage into domestic water sources. Poor access to safe water, poor sanitation and hygiene have been associated with high rates of diseases like diarrhoea, pneumonia, trachoma and worm related illnesses [44, 49].

4.3.2 Adaptation and resilience options

Health adaptation options can be considered on a range of probable technological and behavioural changes such as improved surveillance of infectious epidemic diseases, early warning systems for human health, public health and environmental education, institutional coordination and disaster preparedness and so on [51]. A number of adaptation measures are already being implemented in West African countries. Evidences of implementation of health adaptation measures exist in Gambia, Nigeria

Sierra Leone, Ghana and Guinea Bissau among others. For example Gambia is designing Geographic Information System (GIS) health data bases on several communicable diseases. These user friendly GIS data bases offer real time information and remote data on epidemiological diseases. The country also plans to implement vector control programmes through its proposed investment in public education, social mobilization and an array of preventive measures such as encouragement of use of insecticide treated nets and mosquito repellents [51].

Nigeria has an official National health adaptation strategy guiding the implementation of climate change adaptation in the health sector. Part of the actions being implemented include awareness programme concerning serious health issues that would enable community members to take pre-emptive actions against health challenges [50, 51]. The country is also strengthening its seasonal weather forecasting system through the provision of up to date information on extreme events like dry spells, heavy storms and heat waves, and providing health warnings through the analysis and integration of weather and health threshold data [51].

In Sierra Leone, community health education programmes are providing community health education to enable community members to identify and eliminate breeding sites of disease vectors. The country is also engaging community health workers and volunteers to educate the public in areas of stress management and improved community education in areas of food poisoning, personal hygiene and sanitation [51, 52]. Health sector specific messages, of Sierra Leone's climate change communication strategy under the National Adaptation Plan (NAP), are designed to help reduce health risk associated with climate change. For instance, to address the problem of increasing cases of disease outbreaks resulting from poor sanitation and hygiene, and warmer temperatures, emphasis was placed on educating the people on the need to eradicate vector breeding sites and encourage healthy living in safe environment, and the use of clean and safe water [5].

Ghana also has an official national health adaptation strategy which is guiding programmes' implementation on health adaptation to climate change. Various actions have been implemented, focused on building institutional and technical capacities to work on climate change. In addition, efforts have been directed towards incorporating climate information into integrated disease surveillance and response system, including the creation of early warning and response systems for climate related health risks. Furthermore, programmes have also been implemented to raise resilience of health infrastructure in the country [53].

Other opportunities for action in the sub-region have however been identified. For instance, in the case of Nigeria, WHO/UNFCCC emphasised the need for comprehensive health vulnerability and adaptation assessment incorporating relevant stakeholders from all sectors [50]. The organisations also called for the need to build up institutional and technical capacities in relation to climate change and health, and implementation of activities to increase climate resilience of health infrastructure. In Ghana, WHO/UNFCCC identified the urgent need to conduct a national assessment of climate change impact, vulnerability and adaptation for health in the country, and the need to work on estimating the cost of implementing health resilience to climate change [53]. Furthermore, it was noted that the country had no focal point for climate change in the ministry of health (which is very necessary for proper coordination of programmes and activities).

4.4 Energy

4.4.1 Vulnerabilities and impacts

Increasing population, rapid urbanization and economic growth is pushing up the demand for power in West Africa. However, the sub-region falls within Sub-Saharan Africa which is regarded as the most electricity poor area in the world, where the average electricity rate is about 20%. It is projected that with the present population growth rate, about 500 million will be without electricity by 2040 [49, 54]. The severe shortage of energy has constituted a major constraint to livelihoods and economic development in West African countries. For instance, there is no access to electricity for 80% of the population in Niger, Liberia and Burkina Faso and for 40% in Nigeria (over 70 million) and Senegal [49]. Even for those that have grid connection, supply is grossly unreliable and people as a necessity most often rely on private generators, thereby incurring extra costs. Furthermore, it is observed that electricity tariffs in Africa are among the highest in the world [49, 54].

Millions of people in the sub-region still depend on the traditional use of solid biomass for cooking. Even some people who have access to electricity, liquefied petroleum gas (LPG), natural gas or biogas still continue to use biogas due to cultural or affordability reasons. For instance, Nigeria is included among the five countries (with Ethiopia, DR Congo, Tanzania and Kenya) that account for about half of the Sub-Saharan population using solid biomass for cooking. In the rural areas in particular, majority of households do not have access to clean cooking, they depend on fuel wood and often spend substantial part of the day collecting firewood [54].

The natural vegetation has been considerably destroyed or degraded by agricultural expansion and overexploitation for firewood, charcoal and timber. For instance the natural forest in West Africa has reduced by 37% and with even higher losses in countries like Nigeria, Ghana, Guinea and Sierra Leone [49]. Natural forests are expected to experience significant drop in productivity in the near future, due to rising temperatures and evaporation that will like lead to water balance deficits and reduced productivity in forest resources. The effect will be more in the savannah region which is already experiencing increasing scarcity of wood resources [5, 28–30].

However, more challenges for hydropower development in the sub-region have been projected. It is expected that increased evaporation due to rising temperature, more extreme rainfall events, decreased river flow in some areas, more dam construction and extensive land use changes would cause higher incidents of flood damage to dams, more reservoir evaporation and siltation and increase river flow variability [29, 49].

4.4.2 Adaptation and resilience options

While inadequate electricity constitutes a major constraint to development, more than 50% of West Africa's hydropower potential still remains untapped. Therefore, considering the large number of rivers that can be harnessed for generating electricity, there is still a lot of opportunity for further development of hydropower in the sub-region. There is also s great potential for solar energy and wind power in West Africa. Presently, solar energy plays a limited role in the power sector in Africa in general despite the fact that most parts of the continent enjoy an average of over 320 days/year of sunlight. Thus, potential power generation from solar energy is far greater than present electricity demands and even far into the future [55]. Wind power development is also very limited in West Africa as in other parts of Sub-Saharan Africa, for which the potential is estimated at about 1300 GW. West Africa is considered as one of the areas where the greatest potential for wind power lies in Africa [55].

4.5 Infrastructure

4.5.1 Vulnerabilities and impacts

Basic infrastructural development is generally grossly inadequate in West Africa. Poorly planned settlements, inadequate and poorly constructed roads, dams, bridges, health facilities and so on, creates high vulnerability to weather and environmental risks. There is also disproportionate distribution of infrastructural facilities in favour of urban areas which reduces the accessibility of the rural dwellers to these basic facilities. Massive rural-urban population drift is resulting in rapid urbanization, which is encouraging the spread of informal settlements, particularly in marginal environments like flood plains and other low lying areas, that are highly vulnerable to flooding, sea surges and rising sea level [49, 56]. These extreme weather events are resulting in infrastructure damages (such as for transportation, health, education, energy, water, communication and so on) and disruption of operation. For instance, in the case of transportation rainstorms, flooding, landslides and sea surges disrupts operation and put stress on supply chain capacity and efficiency. Temperature and rainfall trends are further intensifying the problem of inadequate water supply, sanitation and disaster risk management. Flooding during the rainy season and water scarcity during the dry season has become common experience particularly in urban centres in the region. In addition, urban residents in many West African cities now increasingly face health problems associated with urban heat highlands; like heatstroke, cardiovascular and respiratory, diseases, heat exhaustion and dehydration [49].

Coastal cities also face additional problems of sea surges and sea level rise and associated flooding, coastal erosion, inundation and salinization of aquifers. For instance, it is projected that West Africa will likely experience sea level rise of 1 m by 2100, resulting in substantial inundation of many major cities. It is also predicted that by the 2050s annual damages from coastal flooding in the sub-region will be as high as $11billion [49]. In coastal parts of Nigeria, the filling up of some mangrove wetlands for development is already resulting in flooding in many areas and could be worsened by climate-change related accelerated sea level rise. If this situation continues unchecked, about 75% of the population living within 200 km of the coast that derive livelihoods from coastal and marine ecosystems in the country will be affected [57]. It has also been estimated that if there is 2 m rise in sea level, at least 6 million people will be displaced in Lagos alone, while about 80% of people in the Niger Delta will be affected [56, 58].

4.5.2 Adaptation and resilience options

Climate-resilient infrastructure is expected to be planned, designed, constructed and operated in such a way that it projects, prepares for, and adapts to changing climate conditions. It should also be able to withstand and recover quickly from disruptions resulting from extreme weather and climate conditions [59]. Decisions taken on the siting, building and operation of infrastructure give the chance to lessen vulnerability to the physical impacts of climate change. Climate resilience of new or existing infrastructure can be increased by reducing its exposure or sensitivity to climate-related hazards through various adaptation options depending on the existing situation. Adaptation response may involve the implementation of civil engineering measures to protect assets or other measures that may simply require altering maintenance routines or information-sharing practices [60].

Many West African nations have realized the importance of adapting infrastructure to climate change. For instance, in order to secure coastal roads and ports from flooding, sea surges and sea erosion, Togo has made it a priority to adapt its coastal zones to climate change. This has resulted in investments in coastal protection and preventive management actions and increased monitoring and management of coastal erosion [30]. In Ghana, a number of infrastructure adaptation priorities have been identified for water, energy and transport sectors. For instance, technical adaptation for the water sector include maintaining, rehabilitating and re-engineering existing water systems like dams and irrigation systems. It also includes designing and implementing structural adaptation measures like retarding basins, road elevation and provision of culverts. For the energy sector adaptation options includes adoption of climate resilient designs for facilities and good site selection for energy infrastructure. Other actions are integration of climate adaptation into design of transport infrastructure (like use of materials that reflect solar radiation to reduce temperature of pavement), sealing of unpaved roads, improved road drainage design and planting and management of vegetation along roads [61].

One of the main adaptation priorities in Liberia is the development of infrastructure to reduce the vulnerability of urban coastal zones from erosion, floods, siltation and degradation [62]. For instance, coastal defence projects completed in 2015 reduced erosion, siltation, and degraded coastal landscapes around the capital, Monrovia and other areas. Furthermore, importance was placed on implementation of design standards and planning codes for roads and other infrastructure to cope with flooding, sea level rise and windstorms [63]. Liberia's national policy and response strategy on climate change accentuated the integration of climate resilience in the infrastructure sector. Also, aside from stressing the need to improve the use of weather and climate information in infrastructure planning and development, the strategy emphasised the importance of subjecting infrastructure projects (such as roads, ports and airports) to climate risk screening as part of the planning process [64].

5. Recommendations and policy options

Reducing vulnerability and increasing resilience to climate and environmental risks requires developing appropriate adaptation and disaster risk management strategies. Achieving this however depends on proper understanding of the dimensions of exposure and vulnerability and adequate valuation of changes in those dimensions [13]. In addition, building resilience requires identifying possible hazards and understanding the vulnerabilities that may affect recovery from such hazards. Risk information is central to good risk management as it provides the necessary details about what, when and where disasters might occur, how severe it could be and who might be affected. Having an appropriate understanding of the situation provides the opportunity for proper adjustment. Improving adaptation and building resilience require appropriate actions from all actors including communities, governments, NGOs and businesses. Therefore, a number of recommendations on strategies to improve adaption and resilience to climate and environmental risks are provided to guide action at local, national and transnational levels.

5.1 Policy options for local level implementation

1. There is urgent need to raise awareness on climate and environmental risks among the populace. Raising awareness and providing advocacy on climate and environmental risk information is very important in helping people to manage the risk and changes they are facing. Dissemination of information on potential climate and environmental hazards and sharing of knowledge on best practices on climate risk management will play a critical role in improving adaptation and building of resilience. Awareness could be promoted through the formation of climate and environmental risk volunteer corps (CERVC) at community and district levels. The CERVC would be very useful in helping to raise awareness and dissemination of early warning information on climate and environmental risks, and also serve as link between communities and NGOs involved in climate risk actions.

2. Climate and environmental risk should be incorporated into local plans. In addition, development of local community adaptation action plans (LCAAP) should be promoted. This will help in guiding climate and environmental risk action at community level. It will also offer an opportunity for integrating local priorities into regional and national plans.

3. Agricultural extension services should be strengthened and climate-smart agricultural practices, both modern and traditional be encouraged based on the specific environmental conditions in different areas. There is also the need to provide enough personnel, technical equipment and necessary training and re-training that will enable the officials perform efficiently under changing conditions.

4. Individual and communal efforts should be encouraged to promote sustainable management and use of land, water and vegetation resources. In addition, people should be encouraged to form cooperative societies and other local saving and loan associations to improve access to safety nets during crisis periods. Such collective efforts will also help to improve access to inputs like fertilizers, improved seeds and farm chemicals which can be obtained in bulk for distribution. This should be supplemented with government subsidies where possible.

5.2 Policy options for national level implementation

1. National climate and environmental risk assessments should be carried out with emphasis on sectorial and local individualities and priorities, but using the system approach. This approach is necessary because it will help ensure that specific adaptation strategies are not considered in isolation, but as part of wide-ranging concerns that takes cognisance of the interrelatedness and interdependencies within and between all aspects of the environment.

2. Provision of weather and climate information and early warning systems should be introduced where they do not exist and expanded where they are already in operation. In addition to the use of radio services, other technologies like mobile phone services in form of text and voice messages in different local languages can be incorporated. This will ensure regular provision of reliable information on climate and environmental risks, plus possible actions to reduce vulnerabilities. This will also ensure the availability of reliable information on weather and climate-smart agriculture and other adaptation options to the people.

3. National preparedness/contingency/emergency response plans should be formulated and integrated into national development planning and budgeting. This will help expedite action in addressing the impacts of climate change in the different sectors of the economy.

4. Focal points for climate change should be established in all ministries. This will enable proper coordination of programmes and activities in relation to every sector and also ensure easy coordination of actions among ministries and agencies when required.

5. Climate-proofing of infrastructure is very important for building resilience against climate and environmental hazards. Existing transportation, health, education, water, sanitation, waste and other infrastructure should be strengthened to withstand changing conditions. Furthermore, climate change risks should be integrated into the design, operation and management of new infrastructure projects. Technical standards and appropriate legal frameworks incorporating projected climate risks should be introduced and enforced to ensure adherence to such standards in the planning, construction and operation of infrastructural facilities.

5.3 Policy options for transnational level implementation

1. There is need for stronger transnational coordination to address climate change impacts in the sub-region. This could be achieved by mainstreaming climate change adaptation into the numerous ECOWAs policies and programmes. While the improvement of adaptive capacity and resilience to and environmental risks is primarily the responsibility of individual member countries, ECOWAS has an important role to play in developing appropriate policies to regulate actions within the region.

2. Efforts should also be directed at strengthening the numerous sub-regional organizations involved in addressing climate change impacts. These include the various river basin development authorities like the Niger Basin Authority (NBA), Lake Chad Basin Commission (LCBC) and the Organisation for the Development of the Senegal River Basin (OMVS), and other agencies like the West African Science Service Centre on Climate Change Adapted Landuse (WASCAL), Sahel and Sahara Observatory (OSS) and the Permanent Interstate Committee for Drought Control in the Sahel (CILSS). Strengthening these organizations would help to improve adaptation and resilience to climate change across West Africa.

6. Conclusion

In conclusion, the key findings in this research can be summarized as follows:

1. West Africa and in particular the Sahel region has experienced significant environmental change in the last five decades, with great negative implications for agriculture and food security, water resources, human health, energy and infrastructural development;

2. the West African sub-region is susceptible to many climate and environmental risks and the people are highly vulnerable as a result of their social and economic circumstances;

3. great potential exist for raising adaptation and for building resilience in agriculture to ensure food security. Opportunities also exist for improving adaptation and resilience levels in water resources, human health, infrastructure and energy sectors of the economy in the sub-region;

4. achieving sustainable improvement in adaptation and resilience require appropriate actions from multiple stakeholders including communities, governments and NGOs.

This study has therefore provided a foundation for further research. Based on the findings of this research, it is suggested that future research be directed towards:

1. greater understanding of meteorological conditions and generation of necessary climatic data for better prediction and planning;

2. improving adaptive capacity and resilience of under-resourced and marginal population;

3. understanding gender differences in vulnerability in rural and urban areas;

4. the role of public-private partnership in promoting adaptive capacity and resilience.

Funding

This manuscript was not funded by any institution, either public or private.

Conflict of interest

There is no conflict of interests in the preparation of this manuscript.

Code availability

Since the manuscript was based on existing research results, no data/codes are available.

Author details

Bolaji Abdulkadir Usman
Faculty of Social Sciences, Department of Geography and Environmental Management, University of Ilorin, Nigeria

*Address all correspondence to: usman.ba@unilorin.edu.ng

References

[1] Nzuma JM, Waithaka M, Mulwa RM, Kyatalimye M, Nelson G. Strategies for Adapting to Climate in Rural Sub-Saharan Africa: A Review of data Sources, Poverty Strategies (PRSPs) and National Adaptation Plan for Agriculture (NAPAs) in ASARECA Member Countries. IFPRI Discussion Paper No. 01013; 2010. Available from: https://www.ifri.org/publication/strategies-adapting-climate-change-rural-sub-saharan-africa

[2] UNEP. Climate and Environmental Risks and Opportunities in Mexico's Financial System from Diagnosis to Action; 2020. Available from: http://wedocs.unep.org/handle/20.500.11822/34493

[3] Woetzel J, Pinner D, Samandari H, Engel H, Krishnan M, Boland B, Powis C. Climate Risk and Response: Physical Hazards and Socio-Economic Impacts. New York: McKinsey Global Institute; 2020. Available from: https://www.mckinsey.co/business/suatainability/our-insights/climate-risk-and-response-physical-hazards-and-socio-economic-impacts

[4] Malhi Y, Wright J. Spatial patterns and recent trends in the climate of tropical rainforest regions. Philosophical Transactions of the Royal Society of London B. 2004;**359**:311-329

[5] U N D R R. Disaster Risk Reduction in Africa: Status Report-2015; 2016. Available from: https://www.undrr.org/publication/disaster-risk-reduction-africa-status-report-2015

[6] Have C. Our World: Africa and Climate Change. Tokyo: United Nations University; 2008. Available from: https://ourworld.unu.edu/en/africa-and-climate-change

[7] Nicholson S. Land surface processes and Sahel climate. Reviews of Geophysics. 2000;**2002**(38):117-139

[8] USAID. Climate Change Adaptation in Western Africa. Washington, DC: USAID; 2012. Available from: https://www.climatelinks.org/sites/default/asset/document/west_africa_adaptation_fact_sheet_jan2012%20%281%29.pdf

[9] UNCCD. The Global Land Outlook, West Africa Thematic Report. Bonn: UNCCD; 2019 Available from: https://catalogue.unccd.int/1220_GLO_WEST_AFRICA_E.pdf

[10] Jones R. Managing Climate Change Risks. Organization for Economic Cooperation and Development (OECD), Workshop on Benefits of Climate Policy: Improving Information for Policy Makers 12-13 December, 2003; Paris, France; 2003. Available from: https://www.oecd.org/env/cc/19519189.pdf

[11] European Commission. Climate Risk Assessment: An Introduction [Internet]. 2020. Available from: https://europa.eu. [Accessed: December 18, 2021]

[12] Cardona OD, van Aalst MK, Birkmann J, Fordham M, McGregor G, Perez R, et al. Determinants of risk: Exposure and vulnerability. In: Field CB, Barros V, Stocker TF, Qin D, Dokken DJ, Ebi KL, et al. editors. Managing the Risks of Extreme Events and Disasters to Advance Climate Change Adaptation. A Special Report of Working Groups I and II of the Intergovernmental Panel on Climate Change (IPCC), Cambridge, UK, and New York, NY: Cambridge University Press; 2012. pp. 65-108 Available from: https://www.ipcc.ch/assets/uploads/2018/03/SREX-Chap2_FINAL-1.pdf

[13] U N D R R. Understanding Disaster Risk; 2020. Available from: www.preventionweb.net

[14] G F D R R. Understanding risk in an evolving world: Emerging practices in natural disaster assessment; 2014. Available from: www.gfdrr.org

[15] Cutter SL, Boruff BS, Shirley WL. Social vulnerability to environmental hazards. Social Science Quarterly. 2003;**84**(2):243-261

[16] IPCC. Climate Change 2001: Impacts Adaptation and Vulnerability. Contribution of Working Group II to the Third Assessment Report of the IPCC. New York: Cambridge University Press; 2001

[17] IPCC. Climate Change 2014: Impacts Adaptation and Vulnerability. Part A: Global and Sectorial Aspects. Contribution of Working Group II to the Fifth Assessment Report of the IPCC. New York: Cambridge University Press; 2014

[18] Olmos S. Vulnerability and Adaptation to Climate Change: Concepts, Issues and Assessment Methods. Climate Change Knowledge Network, Foundation Paper; 2001. Available from: https://citeseerx.psu.edu/viewdoc/download;sessionid=1FC81C95881D6C9ABEE306E404?doi=10.1.1.119.576&rep=rep1&type=pdf

[19] Ludena CE, Yoon SW. Local Vulnerability Indicators and Adaptation to Climate change: A Survey. Inter-American Development Bank (IDB), Climate Change and Sustainable Division, Technical Notes No. 857. IDB; 2015. Available from: https://publications.iadb.org/publications/english/document/Local-Vulnerability-Indicators-and-Adaptation-to-Climate-Change-A-Survey.pdf

[20] Cornell S, Georgiou T, Kulp M, Yarnal B. Coastal Processes, Hazards, and Society. Dimensions2: Sensitivity. Penn State's College of Earth and Mineral Sciences, Open Education Resources; 2021. Available from: https://www.e-education.psu.edu/earth107/node/733

[21] WHO. Chapter 11: Adaptation and Adaptive Capacity to Lessen Health Impacts. Climate Change and Human Health – Risks and Responses. Geneva, 2003: WHO; Available from: https://www.who.int/globalchange/environment/en/chapter11.pdf

[22] InTeGrate. Module 11.1: Resilience, Adaptive Capacity, and Vulnerability. InTeGrate [Internet]. 2018. Available from: https://serc.carleton.edu/integrate/teaching_materials/foof_supply/student_materials/1059. [Accessed: 16 December 2021]

[23] Usman BA. Vulnerability and adaptation capabilities of the rural poor to climate change challenge in Kwara State, Nigeria. Lapai Sociological Review. 2013;**4**(1):142-162

[24] Burton I, Challenger B, Hug S, Klien RTJ, Yohe G. Adaptation to Climate Change in the Context of Sustainable Development and Equity. Geneva: IPCC; 2018. Available from: https://www.ipcc.ch/site/assets/uploads/2018/03/wg2TARchap18.pdf

[25] United States Department of Health and Human Services National Health Security Strategy. US Department of Health and Human Services; 2009. Available from: https://www.phe.gov/preparedness/planning/nhss

[26] Care International. Adaptation Learning Programme: Climate Change Vulnerability and Adaptive Capacity in

Northern Ghana. Care International/ALP; 2013. Available from: https://careclimatechange.org/wp-content/uploads/2014/08/CVCA_Ghana.pdf

[27] Oguge N, Ayal D, Adeleke I, Silva I. African Handbook on Climate Change Adaptation. Cham: Springer; 2021. Available from: https://library.oapen.org/handle/20.500.12657/49528

[28] Simonsson L. Vulnerability Profile of Burkina Faso. Poverty and Vulnerability Programme. Stockholm: Stockholm Environmental Institute (SEI); 2005 Available from: https://liu.diva-portal.org/smash/get/diva2.225233/FULTEXT01.pdf

[29] USAID. Climate Vulnerabilities and Development in Burkina Faso and Niger: Background Paper. Washington, DC: USAID; 2012 Available from: https://www.climatelinks.org/sites/default/files/asset/document/climate%20Vulnerabilities%20and%20Development%20in%20Burkina%20faso%20and%20Niger.pdf

[30] World Bank. Climate Risk Country Profile: Togo. World Bank Group, Washington, DC; 2021. Available from: https://reliefweb.int/sites/reliefweb.int/resources/15859-WB_Togo%20Country%20Profile-WEB.pdf

[31] Bendandi B, Venier M. Vulnerability and Resilience in West Africa: Understanding Human Mobility in Context of Land Degradation. Global Knowledge Partnership on Migration and Development (KNOMAD), Working Paper No. 25. KNOMAD; 2017. Available from: https://www.knomad.org/sites/default/files/201705/WP%2025_Vulnerability%20resilience%20in%20West%20Africa_1.pdf

[32] UNDP. Africa Adaptation Programme: Niger. New York: UNDP; 2012. Available from: https://www.undp-aap.org/countries/niger

[33] FAO. Save and Grow: A Policy maker's Guide to the Sustainable Intensification of Smallholder Crop Production. Rome: FAO; 2011 Available from: https://www.fao.org/policy-support/tools-and-publications/resources-details/en/c/1421716/

[34] FAO. Climate-Smart Agriculture Sourcebook. Rome: FAO; 2013 Available from: https://www.fao.org/i3325e/i3325e00.htm

[35] Zougmoré R, Partey S, Ouédraogo M, Omitoyin B, Thomas T, Ayantunde A, et al. Toward climate-smart agriculture in West Africa: A review of climate change impacts, adaptation strategies and policy developments for the livestock, fishery and crop production sectors. Agriculture and Food Security. 2016;**5**:26. Available from: https://agricultureandfoodsecurity.biomedcentral.com/track/pdf/10.1186/s40066-016-0075-3.pdf

[36] Sultan B, Gaetani M. Agriculture in West Africa in the Twenty-First century: Climate Change and Impact Scenarios, and Potentials for Adaptation [Internet]. 2016. Available from: https://www.frontiersin.org/articles/10.3389/fpls.2016.0126/full. [Accessed: 17 January 2022]

[37] UNCCD. Science-Policy Interface Land Management and Drought Mitigation. Science Policy Brief. Vol. No. 6. Bonn: UNCCD; 2019. Available from: www.unccd.int

[38] Sanni D, Juanich G. A feasibility study of rice-fish farming in West Africa. In: Halwat M, Van Dam AA, editors. Integrated Irrigation and Aquaculture in West Africa: Concepts, Practices and potentials. Rome: FAO; 2006. pp. 75-78. Available from: https://www.fao.org/3/a0444e/A0444E08.htm#ch6

[39] Peterson J, Kalende M. The potential for irrigation-aquaculture in Mali. In: Halwat M, Van Dam AA, editors. Integrated Irrigation and Aquaculture in West Africa: Concepts, Practices and Potentials. Rome: FAO; 2006. p. 79-94. Available from: https://www.fao.org/3/a0444e/A0444E09.htm#ch7

[40] Peterson J, Kalende M, Sanni D, Ngom M. The potential for integrated irrigation-aquaculture (IIA) in Senegal. In: Halwat M, Van Dam AA, editors. Integrated Irrigation and Aquaculture in West Africa: Concepts, Practices and Potentials. Rome: FAO; 2006. pp. 95-116. Available from: https://www.fao.org/3/a0444e/A0444E10.htm#ch8

[41] USAID. Climate Change and Groundwater Resources in West Africa: Transboundary River Basins. Washington, DC: USAID; 2013 Available from: https://www.climatelinks.org/site/default/files/asset/document/Transboundary%2520River_CLEARED.pdf

[42] UNICEF. Nearly one third of Nigerian children do not have enough water to meet their daily needs-UNICEF [Internet]. 2021. Available from: https://unicef.org/nigeria/press-release/nearly-one-third-nigeria-children-not-have-enough-water-meet-their-daily-needs [Accessed: 12 January 22]

[43] Wetlands International. Guinea Bissau: Mangroves in frontline against climate change [Internet]. 2010. Available from: http://www.wetlands.org/?TabId=60&articleType=ArticleView&articleId=2117 [Accessed: 19 December 21]

[44] New Security Beat. Water Stress, Instability and Violent Extremism in Nigeria [Internet]. 2017. Available from: https://www.newsecuritybeat.org/2017/08/water-stress-instability-violent-extremism-nigeria/. [Accessed: 02 November 2022]

[45] Barry BS, Creeppy EGE, Gacitua-Mario E, Wodon Q. Conflict, Livelihoods, and Poverty in Guinea Bissau. Washington, DC: World Bank; 2007

[46] Anderson ZK. Water Scarcity and Violent Conflict in Nigeria [Master of Arts thesis]. Monterey, CA, USA: Department of Security Studies (Middle East, South Asia, Sub-Saharan Africa), Naval Postgraduate School; 2019. Available from: https://calhoun.nps.edu/bistream/10945/62803/19jun_Anderson_Zach.pdf?sequence=1&isAllowed=y

[47] Japan International Cooperation Agency. Handbook on Climate change Adaptation in the Water Sector: A Resilient Approach that integrates water Management and Community Development. JICA Global Environment Department; 2010. 70 p. Available from: www.jica.go.jp

[48] UN Water. Climate Change and Water: UN-Water Policy Brief. Geneva: UN-Water Technical Advisory Unit; 2019 Available from: https://www.unwater.org

[49] USAID. Factsheet/Climate Risk Profile: West Africa. Washington, DC: USAID; 2018. Available from: https://www.climatelinks.org/sites/default/files/assets/documents/West_Africa_CRP_Find.pdf

[50] WHO and United Nations Convention on Climate Change (UFCCC). Climate and Health Country Profile-2015: Nigeria. Geneva: WHO/UNFCCC; 2015. Available from: https://apps.who.int/iris/handle/10665/208865

[51] Nhamo G, Muchuru S. Climate adaptation in the public health sector in Africa: Evidence from United Nations Framework convention on Climate Change National Communications. Jamba – Journal of Disaster Risk Studies.

2019;**11**(1):a644. DOI: 10.4102/jamba.v11i1.644

[52] Government of Sierra Leone. Sierra Leone's Climate Change Communications Strategy under the National Adaptation Plan. Environmental Protection Agency of Sierra Leone (EPA-SL); 2020. Available from: https://napglobalnetwork.org/wp-content/uploads/2020/10/napgn-en-2020-Sierra-Leone-Climate-Change-Communications-Strategy-under-the-NAP.pdf

[53] WHO and United Nations Convention on Climate Change (UFCCC). Climate and health country profile-2015: Ghana. Geneva: WHO/UNFCCC; 2015. Available from: https://apps.who.int/iris/handle/10665/208862

[54] International Energy Agency. World Energy Outlook 2016. Paris: IEA; 2016

[55] International Energy Agency. Africa Energy Outlook: A Focus on Energy Prospects in Sub-Saharan Africa. World Energy Outlook Special Report. Paris: IEA; 2014

[56] Usman BA, Tunde AM. Climate change challenges in Nigeria: Planning for climate resilient cities. Environmental Issues. 2010;**3**(1):101-110

[57] Federal Republic of Nigeria. National Environmental, Economic and Development Study (NEEDS), for Climate Change in Nigeria (Final Draft). Abuja: Federal Ministry of Environment, Special Climate Change Unit; 2010. Available from: https://unfccc.int/files/adaptation/application/pdf/nigerianeeds.pdf

[58] Metrotra S, Natenzon CE, Omojola A, Folorunsho R, Gilbride J, Rosenzweiig C. Framework for City Risks Assessment: A paper presented at the fifth urban Symposium, Cities and Climate Change: Responding to an Urgent Agenda, June 28-30, 2009, Marseilles, France; 2009. Available from: https://go.worldbank.org/p74DFRD0

[59] OECD. Climate Resilient Infrastructure: Policy Perspectives. OECD Environment Policy Paper No. 14. Organisation for Economic Cooperation and Development (OECD) Environment Directorate, Paris; 2018. Available from: https://www.oecd.org/environment/cc/policy-perspectives-climate-resilient-infrastructure.pdf

[60] Vallejo L, Mullan M. Climate Resilient Infrastructure: Getting the Policies Right. Organisation for Economic Cooperation and Development (OECD), Environment Working Paper No. 121. Paris: OECD; 2017. Available from: https://www.oecdilibrary.org/docserver/02f74d61en.pdf?expires=1633614269&accname=guest&checksum=0070E568BE457B5EFFC415E7202c171

[61] Government of Ghana. Ghana's Adaptation Strategy and Action Plan for the Infrastructure Sector (Water, Energy and Transport Sectors). Ghana: Environmental Protection Agency (EPA); 2020. Available from: https://napglobalnetwork.org/wp-content/uploads/2020/06/napgn-en-2020-Ghana's-Adaptation-Strategy-and-Action-Plan-for-the-Infrastructure-Sector.pdf

[62] USAID. Climate Change Adaptation in Liberia. Washington, DC: USAID; 2012. Available from: https://www.climatelinks.org/sites/default/files/asset/document/liberia_adaptation_fact_sheet_jan2012.pdf

[63] UNDP. National Adaptation Plan in Focus: Lessons from Liberia. UNDP-UN

Environment National Adaptation Plan Global Support Programme (NAP-GSP); 2018. Available from: https://www.idc-climate.org/wpcontent/uploads/2018/07/liberia_nap_country_final_online1.pdf

[64] Republic of Liberia. National Policy and Response Strategy on Climate Change. Monrovia: Environmental Protection Agency of Liberia; 2018. Available from: https://www.epa.gov./r/sites/default/files/National%20Policy%20and%20Response%20Strategy%20on%20Climate%20Change%20Final%20Document-min_0.pdf

Chapter 4

Sources of Social Risks and Risk Management Arrangements

Aman Kiniso

Abstract

Ethiopia's major crises have been caused by institutional failures for which the government is mostly responsible. Institutional and structural flaws are typical causes of governance failure, and they may frequently be traced back to a failed institutional change. The source of social risks in the emerging literatures has not explained by an institutional trap factors. This chapter examines the origins of societal risks, risk management arrangements, and methods for urging institutions to manage risk in Ethiopia. A simple random sampling method were employed to select a total of 382 sampled households from 10 sub-districts. Structured interview schedule, focus group discussion, and key informant interviews data collection tools has been employed. The data were analyzed using principal component analysis and qualitative approach. The result of the qualitative analysis shows social risks faced by households caused from governance failures, institutional disincentives, elite's exploitations, and inefficiency. The result from principal component analysis reveals that market based, informal and public arrangements was identified as institutional arrangements having high factor loadings The imply that institutional arrangements are crucial interventions in managing social risks. Thus, this study suggests a well-designed institution and institutional arraignments for managing risks and removal of the underlying sources of social risks.

Keywords: social risks, institutional traps, risk management, institutional arrangements, and institutional arrangements for social risk management

1. Introduction

Global concerns about multiple risks and uncertainties regarding market volatility, natural disasters, climate change, conflicts, forced displacement have had exacerbated by fears of potential disruptions [1]. In Sub-Saharan Africa specially Ethiopia, social risks have get apparent as one of the most human tragedies. Concerns about the social risk of conflict and mass migration, as well as the most heinous human tragedies, have recently surfaced. Many of the rural peoples in Ethiopia are in a state of crisis. The worst humanitarian crisis and terrible tragedy in Ethiopia are linked to institutional and structural problems for which the government is responsible. Government is responsible in this context means that government corrections may or may not really be a solution or failing to resolve a growing long tradition of institutional problems. These longstanding failures were referred to as institutional traps.

Institutional traps understood as an inefficient but stable institution (norm) [2]. The principal cause for the rise of institutional traps entails institutional inadequacies, security and leadership shortcomings, policies and regulatory inefficiencies, market and institutional failures [2, 3]. These traps, in turn, result in risks particularly in the areas where there is high insecurity. In view of that, Ethiopia's already fragile government systems have been plunged into chaos. As a result, Ethiopia is in a security bind, unable to guarantee basic human rights and address its people's immediate needs. In this sense, Ethiopia's greatest crises have been caused by institutional failures, the majority of which are the government's fault. Typical causes of governance failure are institutional and structural problems, which can often be traced back to a failed institutional reform (norm).

Traditional public policy and welfare economics have assumed that natural disaster, market failures and health problems are common, requiring the intervention of government in order to protect the society. Becks' [4], Risk Society Theory, natural disasters and health problems represented a major concern for the population and society. In this regard, the Cultural theory of Douglas, postulates that "risks caused by structural forces" [5], the governmentality perspective of Foucault [6], conceptualized risk from a new style of governance in modernity. In this regard risk is mainly understood as a concept entirely socially produced.

In the contemporary risk literature, the sources of social risks and risk management have not been well conceived and speculated from institutional perspective explaining institution as rule of the game and institutional arrangement as an intervention for social risk management. This implies that the study of social risks within the notion of institutionalism has been coming behind. Institutions are a part of the social order of society and they govern behavior and expectations of individuals, while at the same time they build social structures and improve social development. According to North [7], throughout history, institutions have been devised by human beings to create order and reduce uncertainty in exchange. Fair institutions ensure that all people have equal rights and a chance to improve their lives, and access to justice when they are wronged [8]. Contrary, study from Latin American and Caribbean (LAC) countries show that the unmet demands of a large share of the population fuel an institutional trap that jeopardizes the sustainability of the social contract.

Most studies carried out in eastern Ethiopia, focused on the risks of climate change, conflict, food insecurity. Moreover, poor governance and weak capacity were also contributed to slow progress of drought-risk management in Ethiopia [9]. In study area smallholder households were extensively exposed to social risks of food insecurity and production loss [10], illegal and forced displacement and migration CISP [11]; price rises, illness, job loss, underemployment, deaths, and injustices. Empirically, in social protection landscape of Ethiopia, studies mainly focused PSNP of public arrangements of social risk management. Cash- and food-for-work Productive Safety Net Programme (PSNP), which constitutes a key part of the government's Food Security Programme (FSP). Nevertheless, the PSNP is not the only policy arrangement that aims to provide a form of social protection in rural Ethiopia [12]. The challenges in operationalization of national social protection policy in Ethiopia compounded with inadequate coordination arising from institutional capacity imbalance. This, in particularly, hampered by a lack of limited vertical interface, frequent changes of institutional arrangements, and imbalance between government agencies [13]. Overall, few studies have examined the institutional trap factors of social risks and social risk management arrangements.

This book chapter argue that institutional traps caused from longstanding failures if not well managed can easily be transformed into social risks. Given this, the source of social risks in the emerging literatures has not explained by an institutional trap factors. Yet, if it is possible to be acquainted with a persistent institutional force, it can be considered the "institutional trap as a cause of social risks. The solution to this crisis is to design effective institutional arrangements (social risk management), but there is no consensus on what those institutional arrangements are. Moreover, the failure to establish, devise, and deliver adequate social protection solutions necessitates an understanding of contemporary institutional causes of social risks as well as the role of institutional arrangements in social risk management. Conceptualizing and assessing the matters of social risks from institutional perspectives may provide a means for simultaneously managing the multiple social risks through institutional arrangements would be significant to get lessons for the study area. The contributions of the present paper thus to provide an empirical account of institutional dynamics that may explain the underlying causes of a social risks and risk management arrangements in Ethiopia. The objective of this chapter thus examines the origins of societal risks, risk management arrangements, and methods for urging institutions to manage risk in Ethiopia.

2. Sources of social risks and risk management arrangements

2.1 Institutional traps as a sources of social risks

Social risks and deprivations suffered by the poor have resulted from a long tradition of institutional traps. Given this, the causal instruments of social risks were related to the nation of institutional traps. In this case, institutions, primarily institutional traps further trigger the impossibility of access to social risk management. Such interlinked traps are particularly relevant in a rapidly changing pastoral landscape, which poses new and increasingly complex social risks. In this subsection, four institutional traps that caused social risks were generated by employing focused group discussion and key informant interviews. These are governance failures, institutional disincentives, elite's exploitations, and inefficiency.

2.1.1 Governance traps of social risk

Respondents explained governance failures, administrative injustices, and the resulting human rights violations committed by various actors (civilian administrative officials, polices, and federal military) contributed to social risks in the study areas (**Table 1**). This was explained in terms of territorial centralization of government context and delayed government intervention to maintain social stability and partial federal security treatments, especially from 2016 to 2019. For instance, on September 01, residents of Mieso woreda engaged in daylong fighting with members of the "Liyu Police". The clash left "more than 30 people dead and several others injured. The government became very weak and fragile as of post-September 2017 in Oromia and Somali regions where many fatalities occurred, scores injured, thousands displaced, and livestock worth millions of Birr driven away. One informant from Dire Kale kebele of Gumbi-Bordode district stated "when cattle were looted, rape, and killings committed by bandits openly supported by the Liyu Police, federal army and police not intervene immediately". These show how imperfect political agency together with army bias and weak accountability strengthen each other and

No.	Indicators	Consequences/risks
1.	Delay and weak government intervention	Spark insecurity/instability and erupted deadly conflicts
2.	Absence of state cooperation (Oromia and Somali region)	Worsened security issues and lawlessness including contraband trades Contributes to the eruption of conflicts mobilized and forced them to bear arms
3.	Worsened supremacy of law	prevalence of criminal activities and peoples to acquire arms at a soaring price
4.	Worsened supremacy of law	prevalence of criminal activities and peoples to acquire arms at a soaring price

Table 1.
Risks induced by governance and administrative injustices.

undermine or disrupt the chance of cooperation between elites and communities. According to Ortiz et al. [14], the presences of natural resources weakens or corrupts government, leads to a lack of transparency and accountability, and provoke internal conflicts, which lead to additional scope for mismanagement. This risk is referred to as "governance risk".

According to the leader of Fayo kebele of Mieso district, there were recurrent occurrences of insecurity; the causes pressed out are failure of negotiation and agreement to end "border hostilities" between Oromo and Somali. He further stated citing the agreement signed by presidents of Somali and Oromia regional states to end "border hostilities" in April 2017. After three months, the locals have increasingly become resentful of the extrajudicial stretch by members of the "Liyu Police". This implies the failure of interstate cooperation was the root factor for the eruption of deadly conflicts in the woredas and thereby contributed to the absence of supremacy of law. Similarly, land grabs eviction of farmers around Finfinnee and the fears that a plan to expand the capital into the Oromia region is giving for the birth of Oromo political protests. In response to this, in the study area, the government inhumanely cracking down on people, attacks committed by local militia, Afar Special Police Forces, special Militia (Liyu. Hayli) of the Somali region, and the Ethiopia Defense Forces, since the beginning of 2015, resulted in for 102 civilian causalities, mass migration, displacement, and massive human rights abuse. The public's trust in the government continues to be historically low, mainly for protesters victims of extrajudicial killing by security forces, labeling protesters as terrorists and anti-development forces.

Massive displacement and the sudden deportation of Oromo is another challenge in the study area. They were displaced and deported from the Somali region, Djibouti, and currently settled in Bordode, Asabot, and Mieso as well as in new settlement sites across the Oromia region. Migration from study area through the eastern migratory routes transiting through Djibouti, Somaliland, and Yemen, and the sudden arrival of deported migrants and the linked risks of abuse such as violence, rape, and outright murder, and risks of dehydration, starvation, extortion, robbery and sexual abuse was reportedly expressed by women returnee during focused group discussion. The driving forces are a) conflict; b) political threats (opposition/protest in Oromia region presented a severe threat to regime interests) and c) lack of government willingness to redress incidences of insecurity for the last two decades has contributed for social risks to happen.

2.1.2 Institutional disincentives

Institutional indicators of livelihood include ownership and rights over productive assets, access to rural financial markets, and access to credit services. In certain circumstances, access to and effective arrangements is the most important incentive for pastoralists in securing a livelihood. Observing experiences of diverse parts of the world, Bonfoh et al. [12] argue that mobility is vital for many pastoral communities in securing their livelihoods. In the study area, respondents revealed that the ineffectiveness of rules or arrangements were institutional traps resulted in livelihood risks. Lack of property rights to access credit and pasture depletion and rangeland degradation are strong factors that drive the households and members of the household's movement to search for better livelihood means. The weakening adaptive capacity of customary institutions in the face of adversity, and threats or significant sources of stress result in the rise of new arrangements of land use that leads to resource degradation and disputes between users. Constraints to sustainable pastoral development include little and misdirected public and private investment, weak resource rights, a lack of human capital, an ineffective pastoral voice, and poor governance [15].

The evidence of findings on sources of livelihood risks that comes mainly from focus group discussants in the study area entails pasture depletion, limited livelihood; disputes over pasture and water resources; increased input costs; migration; and food insecurity. This was directly triggered by the weakness of institutions and arrangements. For instance, depletion of pasture and water resources destabilize the pastoral livestock production system and in turn declined yield and also affected livelihood outcome. One of the kebele leaders in the area responded that their matter was not only limited to pasture depletion and water shortage but also the limited capacity of our customary institutions and inadequate or absence of legal instruments for pasture management. Poor are vulnerable households, communities, and those highly entrapped by risks of livelihood. Finding of Sujakhu et al. [16] indicated that limited adaptive; lack of human capital and natural capital limits livelihood diversification options and the opportunity for a higher income. Lower revenue and savings were also other factors that limit financial capital.

Furthermore, interviewers addressed that remoteness and incidences of insecurity restrict access to financial services and market-based social protection of food security; and inequitable access to productive assets again restrained livestock production performance and coupled with the nature of communal ownership of land in the pastoral area together. Where livelihood diversification becomes challenging following Tenaw [17] study, the inability of pastoral and agro-pastoral communities to diversify their livelihoods was due to poor asset base, lack of financial facilities, lack of awareness and training, lack of rural infrastructure, and lack of opportunities. Increased input costs, migration, and food insecurity are also other risks that lead to losses of livelihood assets. Undoubtedly, weak social institutions restrict formal credit access and prolonged inadequate access to income can lead to livelihood risk.

The expansion of cultivated lands and increased competition for natural resources resulted in increased security and transhumance problems pastoralists' face. Indeed, pastoralists fall to reach their potential due to legal, economic, social, and political disincentives and barriers to the mobility of livestock and communal management of rangelands. In the area, the emerging land-use system (dryland agriculture) and lacking legal ownership of rangeland restricted livestock mobility to seek pasture and water and in turn, mobility seems to be a source of livelihood insecurity. Haller et al. [18] argues that pastoral commons are under increasing pressure from overuse, land management policies, the persistent misconception of pastoralism, and combined with increasing land alienation and fragmentation.

Institutional disincentives producing unjustly high livelihoods risks mainly relate to institutional failures as explained by respondents. These include the absence of operational capacity, bad governance, limited access to credit, and unpleasant interactions between cultivators and pastoralists. This study coincides with that of Azlina and Bakar [19] that highlighted that institutional disincentives depressed livelihoods and local hostility toward park establishment. This was due to the failure of institutions (institutional arrangement of TSMP) to provide incentives conditions for instance promoting alternatives livelihoods, integrating local customary institutions, and building trust and social capital among stakeholders.

2.1.3 Elites and security forces exploitation

Elites dominance and biased in the study area described as a cause of social instability through control over natural, economic, political, social, organizational, symbolic (expertise/knowledge) resources, stand in a privileged position to formally or informally influence decisions and practices that have broad societal impact. This can be done through the elite's networks. Elite networks are a set of elite actors that jointly control and share resources. Networks may be local or national and they are increasingly transnational and often tightly connected across the various level. Weak institutions allow government officials to engage in self-serving opportunism that increases transaction costs for others and dissipates government funds, thus making the social policy less predictable. Moreover, the damage to economic prosperity and the risks to human development and welfare in failing states and those in which corruption is deeply embedded among ruling elites. The massive human welfare problem, resource constraints, and weak public institutions pose a dilemma for state-based social security systems. Because formal social security schemes primarily help those who are already privileged by having secure jobs and steady incomes and exclude those whose needs for social protection are the greatest, an extension of social security schemes may be regressive and contribute negatively to the security of the very poor [20].

Weak governance adversely affects socio-political stability, income and employment opportunities, and sustained settlements of people. People can be dissatisfied with their life if they lose their lives, lose use and ownership rights over tangible and intangible resources that determine their collective identity and dignity. Corrupt practices or the failure of institutions that protect legitimate rights, weak governance, weakness collective action, and weak political representations in policy-making processes exacerbates social discontents, political unrest, and economic instability. Following Oromo Protests torch has been committed local officials including security. In both districts, instability and social discontent over the local governments are explained. Recently, rising levels of citizen dissatisfaction with public services and institutions lead to socio-political instability across the globe. Understanding the underlying causes of multifaceted social discontent, civil unrest and protests help address the structural sources of discontent. Referring to the work of Sebastián et al. [21] structural challenges, lack of trust in institutions, and inclusivity in dialog considered drivers of social discontent that undermine citizens' prospects of well-being.

2.1.4 Inefficient social protection arrangements

One of the main reasons why social welfare institutions exist is taking care of people and to pool and redistribute social risks. This includes community organizations, political groups, and churches. However, they also include information resources such as friends, neighborhood networks, and social support groups. Welfare institutions of households of the study area and the natural ecosystem over which subsistence livestock production performed for their immediate subsistence needs rather than demands of a market are closely linked to each other. Informal welfare of afosh/idir, guza/debo, hirpha, free use of pack animals; gift-giving and credit without interest from social networks; transfers from mutual support networks revealed as common institutions, were pastoralists and agro-pastoralists mainly relied on upon response to multifaceted risks and also serves as social-economic problems solving arrangements. Drivers are lack value-added marketing, depletion of pasture together with water and scarcity of grazing land, interferences of brokers in livestock marketing, pastoral communities' dissatisfaction with public social goods, and service delivery induced by corruption. Lacks adequate access to social protection in rural encompass a lack of legal entitlements, informal nature, and type of employment, low contributory capacity. Fiscal constraints and weak administrative capacity have also limited the reach of social protection programs to poor rural areas [22].

2.2 Institutional arrangements for social risk management

This subsection presented and discussed types of institutional arrangements for social risk management. To discuss institutional arrangements for social risk management, one needs to understand the categories/types of the existing institutional arrangements in the study area that households' used to manage social risks. Institutional arrangements understood as the Institutional arrangements are the combination of formal constraints, informal rules, and their enforcement characteristics [23]. Institutional arrangements for social risk management is defined as institutional arrangements for dealing with risk through informal (family or community-based), market based and publicly-provided mechanisms [24]. It is also explained as an informal, market, and public based arrangements that help individuals and households to help manage social risks. Informal arrangements for social risk management: These include marriage, mutual community support, and savings in real assets such as cattle, real estate, and gold. Market-based arrangements for social risk management: These include financial assets - cash, bank deposits, bonds, and shares - and insurance contracts. Publicly mandated or provided arrangements: These include social insurance, transfers, and public works.

Smallholder crop and livestock producers' perceptions of institutional arrangement for social risk management for 22 variables were run using the principal component analysis to determine the number of components and to produce dependent variables for the multivariate regression model used for determinants of institutional arrangements for social risk management. A summary of the analysis is given in **Table 2** indicated that the KMO = 0.89 was greater values as the value is well above the acceptable limit of 0.5. The Barlett's Test of Sphericity produced a p-value = 0, which is smaller than 0.01 and thus indicates a significant correlation structure supporting the appropriateness of component analysis for the data. Three components with Eigenvalues greater than 1 indicate relatively large amounts of variance with a cumulative percentage of 76.39 were presented and summarized in **Table 2**.

Component loadings greater than 0.50 and high communalities were considered for the interpretation of the principal components.

Component 1 was named 'market arrangements'. The idea of naming market arrangement comes from the loadings of saving and lending services from rural savings and credit cooperative (RUSACCOP); contract farming/marketing (CANTFRM); marketing linkages and services from multipurpose cooperatives (MULTCOOP); saving and lending services from microfinance institutions (MFIS); micro and small-scale enterprise (MICRENTP); and saving and lending services from village savings and loan association (VSLA). As can be observed from results presented in **Table 2**, component 1 is strongly relevant to risk impact sharing mechanisms represented by an array of the market (saving, credit, lending service, and marketing). Additionally, high loadings of

Institutional Arrangement	**Mean**	**SD**	**Factor loadings**			
			Comp1	**Comp2**	**Comp3**	**Communality**
1. FREEOXEN	2.57	1.542	0.65	0.52		0.78
2. FREPACK	1.88	2.895		0.73		0.54
3. GIFTGIV	1.71	1.904		0.93		0.88
4. MUTALSUP	2.60	1.746		0.73		0.62
5. CUSTTENU	1.68	1.810		0.95		0.91
6. COMMFINC	2.68	1.696	0.73			0.76
7. MULTCOOP	2.44	1.532	0.84			0.72
8. MFI	2.58	1.461	0.88			0.81
9. RUSACCOP	2.65	1.503	0.91			0.87
10. VSLA	2.58	1.484	0.83			0.77
11. LABORMKT	2.48	1.577	0.76			0.72
12. MICRENTP	2.60	1.525	0.83			0.77
13. CANTFRM	2.62	1.433	0.87			0.76
14. RETAILER	.90	1.090		0.77		0.61
15. POS	2.13	1.715	0.76			0.68
16. CASHPW	2.42	1.661	0.71			0.60
17. FOODPW	2.99	1.389			0.89	0.86
18. CASHPER12	2.49	1.788	0.59		0.71	0.89
19. FODTER12	2.88	1.406			0.88	0.91
20. CASHTEM6	1.42	1.770		0.86		0.88
21. FODTEM6	1.41	1.736		0.87		0.83
22. RESETLE	1.53	1.887		0.80		0.64
Eigenvalues			9.29	5.82	1.70	
Variance explained%			35.11	27.46	13.82	
Cumulative %			35.11	62.57	76.40	

Note: The correlation was suitable analysis (P < .001; KMO = 0.895).

Table 2.
Mean, standard deviation and varimax factor of institutional arrangement.

multiple scopes of teamwork were noticed. This component accounts for nearly 35.1% of the total variation. Individual households will also take advantage of market-based institutions such as money, banks, and insurance companies when they are available. However, given these instruments' limitations due to market failure, their usage will be initially restricted but will rise with financial market development. Because formal market institutions are reluctant to lend to households without secured earnings, microfinance is also an important instrument of social risk management.

Component 2 is called 'informal arrangements' because of the significant loadings of risk management arrangement related to free use of pack animals (camels or donkeys) (FREPACK); gift-giving and credit without interest from social networks (GIFTGIV); transfers from mutual support networks (MUTALSUP); customary land tenure systems reduce risk of social conflicts (CUSTTENU); and resettlement with access to enough farmland (RESETLE). On the component 'informal arrangement', relatively high loadings of an arrangement of gift-giving and credit without interest from social networks, and customary land tenure systems were accompanied with high loadings of arrangements that are required by informal arrangements of social risk management. Using free use of pack animals, transfers from mutual support networks and resettlement with access to enough farmland, all of these instruments are needed in case of risk management through an informal arrangement. Component two explains about 27.46% of the total variation of households' informal risk management arrangements. Informal arrangements have existed since the dawn of humankind and still constitute the main source of risk management for the majority of the world's population. In the absence of market institutions and public provisions, the way that individual households respond to risk is to protect themselves through informal (family or community) or personal arrangements (self-protection and self-insurance).

According to an understanding generated from key informants and focused group discussants, informal arrangements are organizations/groups of people for solidarity, predominantly instituted to govern their relationship through customary laws that serve people in solving their various political and social, economic, and environmental matters. These include afosh/idir, farmer's association, guza/debo, and hirpha are mutual help for households exposed to and severely affected by different risks.

Afosha/Idiris traditional organization of people for solidarity, mainly established to celebrate funerals and support the families of the deceased. Discussants described afosha as a helpful arrangement that provides bits of help and a service (food, credit, and moral incentives) during the wedding, funerals, loss of property crisis faced members, and also provides non-members in case they faced social problems, for example, supporting displaced people. In lining with this, the work of the Oromia regional task force [25] on a program of the plan on adaptation to climate change reported that community-based organizations (such as Afosha/Idir), support members during emergencies and also provide credits during the crisis. Other studies also narrated "afosha" generally used for solidarity purposes among neighbors: support a family after death, wedding expenses, and maintenance of the mesquite [26]. Others argue that 'Idir' and 'Afosha' are mainly established to formalize funerals and to help support the families of the deceased and also used for labor sharing and development purposes [27].

Farmer associations arranged on matters concerning natural and productive resources, sociopolitical and economic as well as development issues of their kebeles that influence the livelihoods of fellow/member villagers at village levels. According to focused group discussion participants, road construction, natural resource management and decision on kebeles administrative are issues and tasks undertaken by the household's participation. Aregu et al. [27] claims that farmers' association as a semi-autonomous entity that is directly involved in decisions regarding the land, water, natural resources, and other productive, social, and political issues that affect the lives of all community members.

Guza is labor sharing arrangement and non-reciprocal workgroup that comes together to help each other through labor sharing for farmland preparation, house construction, and other works. This arrangement was considered as helpful according to participants of focused group discussion. It provides help to households' during family labor shortage and in case of death, illness faced households' labor force and member leave to attend education, and also migrate/move to other places far from family for a socio-economic purpose. On the contrary Borchgrevink et al. [28] argued that there is a change that the caller/landowner is no longer responsible to provide the food and drink. This implies that the guza institution was reconstituted so that each member of the work team brought their food, drink, and khat, and the team rotated, working on each other's land.

In the study area, social assistance (Hirpha/gargaarsa) is another arrangement of mutual help for households. This social assistance arrangement is a mechanism for managing risks. In Mieso and Gumbi-Bordode district pastoralists supported displaced people and people who lost their property due to damages as a result of border conflicts and vulnerable sections of member villagers through hirph/gargaarsa arrangement. This implies that hirpha/gargaarsa is one of the mechanisms in which vulnerable people are supported because of customary laws urge mutual support systems. Confirmatory with the understandings generated from participants of focused group discussion, one study in Madda Walabu, argued that Hirpha is the main coping strategy for resilience from shocks and extensive support system for specific vulnerable members of their community such as orphans, the disabled, and women with many unproductive children [29].

Component three was labeled 'public arrangements' with high loadings for three of transfer aspects: food transfer from public work project/program (FOODPW), cash transfer from permanent direct support (12 months) program (CASHPER12), and food transfer from permanent direct support (12 months) program (FODTER12). They seem to be more helpful in response to income and food insecurity shocks. Public arrangements are interventions or mandates of the government to provide (social) insurance programs for risks such as unemployment, old-age, work injury, disability, widowhood, and sickness. On the other hand, governments have a whole array of instruments to help households to cope after a shock hits, such as social assistance, subsidies on basic goods and services, and public work programs [30]. Public arrangements for dealing with risk came into being with the development of the modern welfare state but are relatively scarce and have very limited coverage in the developing world for fiscal and other reasons. When informal or market-based risk management arrangements do not exist, break down, or are dysfunctional, the government can provide or mandate social insurance programs for risks such as unemployment, old-age, work injury, disability, widowhood, and sickness [31]. Institutional and governance risks refer to those posed by interacting with financial institutions, the government (regulatory environment), and conflict. Poor governance may affect the capacity of people to access and maintain assets, services, and utilities. It may also lead to increased transaction costs associated with investments.

In the study area, the most widely used public arrangements are limited to a productive safety-net program. The Productive Safety Net Programme (PSNP) in

Ethiopia was set up in 2005 by the government as part of a strategy to address chronic food insecurity. The PSNP provides cash or food to people who have predictable food needs in a way that enables them to improve their livelihoods and therefore become more resilient to the effects of shocks in the future [32]. PSNP was launched to smooth consumption of chronically food insecure households by providing transfers of cash and/or food during lean months to address both the immediate and underlying causes of food insecurity.

As per the result from key informants, benefiting from a productive safety net program of social protection is difficult due to bias and corruption on the poor to be included and part of PSNP. This was mainly correlated with the lack of transparency in client selection from local governments, development agents, and expertise working on food and nutritional security position in the districts. Moreover, one of my key informants (development agent) serving on the position of animal science at kebele/sub-district level seriously pointed out the challenges they faced from beneficiaries and local government agents during the implementation of PSNP particularly on the selection of target group. From the side of households/communities, most households refused to register their wealth correctly and increase the number of family members for the sake of grasping PSNP opportunity. Whereas, unfair use of power by members of local government working at the community level that, resulted in the exclusion of poor people from PSNP benefits. This means that local leaders and members of the governmental body decided beneficiaries without the active involvement of the community. The result of discussions of focused group discussion and from most focused group discussion showed that relational and favors approaches/arrangements in the productive safety-net program together with lack of community participation and political intervention in the productive safety-net program considered as a challenge that undermined the possibilities of poor households' inclusion.

Along with this, the study that was undertaken by Weltaji et al. [33] indicated that the practice of PSNP was challenged by a lack of monitoring and evaluation of structures, low payment, and limited awareness of beneficiaries. While, the study from Berlie [34] argued that premature graduation, lack of transparency in targeting, and delay transfer of safety nets were the major challenges encountered by the beneficiary female-headed households. Poor geographical, administrative, and community targeting and also the process of targeting the poor is froth with nepotism, corruption as demonstrated by the high inclusion ratio of non-poor households in the program [35]. Other challenges that negatively affect the program include weak institutional linkages and a lack of active community participation in the decision making process.

3. Conclusion

In this chapter institutional traps that caused social risks and institutional arrangements for social risk management in pastoral and agro pastoral areas has examined thoroughly. In view of that, governance failures, institutional disincentives, elite's exploitations, and inefficiency were explored as major institutional traps causes of social risks. Risks of human death, loss of property and new version of gun attacks against people and a long run cumulative effects of socio-political instability, border issues, government armed forces attacks and lack good governance has intensified and resulted for over 1 million Oromo people displacement from Somali regions and Djibouti in general and thousands of people displaces, more hundred injured and deaths of many people was also evidenced in the study area.

To manage such social risks, households in the study area used an informal, market, and public arrangement. The findings imply that institutional arrangements are crucial interventions in managing social risks. Thus, this study suggests a well-designed institution and institutional arraignments for ensuring tenure security and removal of the underlying sources of social risks and challenges thereby help the creation of sustained social protection in the area.

In this regard, future research should focus on exploring a more sustainable social risk management strategy through institutional perspectives and could investigate how social risk management arrangements be institutionalized in the day to day life from a dynamic perspective.

Conflict of interest

The authors declare no conflict of interest.

Author details

Aman Kiniso
Oda Bultum University, Chiro, Ethiopia

*Address all correspondence to: kena5406@gmail.com

References

[1] Jorgensen SL, Siegel PB. Social protection in an era of increasing uncertainty and disruption. Social Protection in an Era of Increasing Uncertainty and Disruption. 2019. DOI: 10.1596/31812

[2] Polterovich VM. Institutional Traps and Transition. CEMI RAS Working Paper. 1999. pp 1-21. Available from: http://dx.doi.org/10.2139/ssrn.1751835

[3] OECD/ECLAC/CIAT/IDB. Revenue Statistics in Latin America and the Caribbean. Paris: OECD Publishing; 2018. DOI: 10.1787/rev_lat_car-2018-en-fr

[4] Beck U. Risk Society: Towards a New Modernity. London: SAGE; 1992

[5] Douglas M. Risk and Blame: Essays in Cultural Theory. London: Routledge; 1992

[6] Foucault M. Governmentality. In: G. Burchell and et al, editors. The Foucault Effect. 1991. pp. 87-104

[7] North, Douglas C. "Economic performance through time." Mary C. Brinton/VictorNee Eds. In: The New Institutionalism in Sociology; Stanford: Stanford University Press; 1998. p.247-257

[8] OECD. Building more effective, accountable, and inclusive institutions for all. OECD Post. 2015;**6**(1):1-16. http://www.oecd.org/dac/_POST-2015

[9] Duguma MK, Brüntrup M, Tsegai D. Policy Options for Improving Drought Resilience and its Implication for Food Security: The Cases of Ethiopia and Kenya, Studies. Vol. 98, ISBN 978-3-96021-056-6. Bonn: Deutsches Institut für Entwicklungspolitik (DIE); 2017

[10] Gemechu F, Zemedu L, Yousuf J. Determinants of farm household food security in Hawi Gudina district, west Hararghe zone, Oromia regional state, Ethiopia. Woodpecker Journal of Agricultural Research. 2015;**4**(6):66-74. DOI: 10.5897/JAERD2014.0660

[11] CISP. Committee for the Development of people CISP Financial Statement for the Year Ended 31 December 2017. CISP analysis Audit 2017 Finale.pdf. 2018

[12] Lavers T. Food security and social protection in highland Ethiopia: Linking the productive safety net to the land question. Journal of Modern African Studies. 2013;**51**(3):459-485. DOI: 10.1017/S0022278X13000402

[13] Hailu D, Northcut T. Ethiopia's social protection landscape: Its surface and underlying structures. International Social Work. 2013;**56**(6):828-846

[14] Ortiz I, Schmitt V, and De L. 100 years of social protection: The road to universal social protection systems and floors Volume I: 50 country cases: Vol. I. 2019. https://www.ilo.org/wcmsp5/groups/public/ed_protect/soc_sec/documents/publication/wcms_669790.pdf

[15] Bonfoh B, Zinsstag J, Fokou G, et al. Pastoralism at the crossroads: New avenues for sustainable livelihoods in semiarid regions. In: Wiesmann U, Hurni H, editors. With an International Group of co-Editors. Research for Sustainable Development: Foundations, Experiences, and Perspectives. Perspectives of the Swiss National Centre of Competence in Research (NCCR) North-South. Vol. 6. Bern, Switzerland: University of Bern; 2011. pp. 549-570

[16] Sujakhu NM, Ranjitkar S, Niraula RR, Asad M, Nizami A, Schmidt-vogt D, et al. Determinants of livelihood vulnerability in farming communities in two sites in the Asian highlands. Water International. 2018;**43**(2):165-182. DOI: 10.1080/02508060.2017.1416445

[17] Tenaw ZT. Constraints of pastoral and agro-pastoral livelihood diversification in eastern Ethiopia: The case of Mieso District. Oromia Regional State. 2016;**4531**:267-274

[18] Haller T, Van Dijk H, Bollig M. Conflicts, security and marginalization: Institutional change of the pastoral commons in a 'glocal' world. Revue Scientifique et Technique (International Office of Epizootics). 2016;**35**(2):405-416. https://doi.org/10.20506/rst.35.2.2532

[19] Azlina N, Bakar A. The Importance Arrangements for Sustainable Livelihoods: The Case of Tun Sakaran Marine Park. 2015

[20] Verpoorten R, and Verschraegen G. Formal and informal social protection in sub-Saharan Africa: A complex welfare mix to achieve poverty and inequality reduction. Status: Published, January 2008, 1-26. 2008

[21] Sebastián NP, Mario P, Juan V. OECD Development Centre. Social discontent in Latin America through the lens of development traps. 2019. Available from: https://oecd-development-matters.org/2019/12/23/social-discontent-in-latin-america-through-the-lens-of-development-traps/

[22] Allieu A. Implementing nationally appropriate social protection systems and measures for all : gaps and challenges facing rural area. 2019. https://www.un.org/development/desa/dspd/wpcontent/uploads/sites/22/2019/03/Andrew-Allieu_SP-for-rural-areas_22-Feb-18.pdf

[23] North DC. Understanding the Process of Economic Change. Princeton: Princeton University Press; 2005

[24] Holzmann, Kozel. The role of social risk management in development: A world bank view. Institute of development studies. Bulletin. 2007;**38**:3

[25] Oromia National Regional State Task Force. Oromia National Regional State: Program of plan on adaptation to climate change. 2011. Available from: https://www.academia.edu/32904711/Oromia_National_Regional_State_Program_of_Plan_on_Adaptation_to_Climate_Change_Team_Members_Participated_in_this_Document_Preparation_Regional_Task_force_Members

[26] Allaverdian C. Innovation and collective action in managed irrigation schemes a first rank resource to land and water scarcity. 2007

[27] Aregu L, Bishop SC, Puskur R. Opportunities for promoting gender equality in rural Ethiopia through the commercialization of agriculture. Improving Productivity and Market Success of Ethiopian Farmers Project (IPMS). Working Paper No. 18. Addis Ababa, Ethiopia. 2010;**18**:1-68

[28] Borchgrevink A, Poutiainen P. Evaluation of Cash for Relief Intervention in Ethiopia -Usaid. November 2004. Available from: http://pdf.usaid.gov/pdf_docs/PDACD354.pdf

[29] RPLRP (Regional Pastoral Livelihood Resilience Project). Pastoral Community Development Project PCDP-3 and Regional Pastoral Livelihood Resilience Project (RPLRP) Social Assessment Report (Final). 2013. Available from: https://doi.org/10.1017/CBO9781107415324.004

[30] Holzmann R. Social Protection Discussion Paper Series Risk and

Vulnerability: The Forward Looking Role of Social Protection in a Globalizing World Risk and Vulnerability: The forward looking role of social protection in a globalizing. Risk Management 0109. 2001.

[31] Robert H, Lynne SB, Emil T. Social Risk Management: The World Bank's Approach to Social Protection in a Globalizing World. 2003

[32] HPN (Humanitarian Practice Network). Special Feature: The Crisis in the Horn of Africa.53. 2012. Available from: http://odihpn.org/wpontent/uploads/2012/03/humanitarianexchange053

[33] Welteji D, Mohammed K, Hussein K. The contribution of Productive Safety Net Program for food security of the rural households in the case of Bale Zone, Southeast Ethiopia. Agriculture and Food Security. 2017;**6**:53. DOI: 10.1186/s40066-017-0126-4

[34] Berlie AB. The role of productive safety net Programme (PSNP) in improving female-headed Households' food security: The case of Enebsie Sar Midir District of the Amhara region, Ethiopia. Eastern Africa Social Science Research Review, Project MUSE. 2018;**34**(1):109-136. DOI: 10.1353/eas.2018.0003

[35] Nigussa, F, Mberengwa I. Challenges of Productive Safety Net Program implementation at local level: The case of Kuyu Woreda, North Shewa Zone, Oromia Region, Ethiopia. Journal of Sustainable Development in Africa. 2009;**11**(1):248-267

Section 3

Leadership

Chapter 5

Communication and Leadership for Improving ERM Effectiveness

Thomas Wolter

Abstract

Many companies implementing Enterprise Risk Management (ERM) struggle with its effectiveness. Available studies of risk practitioners' practices describe and categorise phenomena related to establishing ERM. This qualitative study uses a cross-sectional field design to explore risk practitioners' communication and leadership practices for achieving and maintaining effectiveness. It forms a practical guide for risk practitioners to manage ERM effectiveness and for organisations to optimise risk development programs. Risk practitioners apply four practice episodes—the first aims at creating shared knowledge and meaning. The second episode emphasises the value-creating capabilities of the organisational ERM. Leadership, the third practice episode, aims at increasing influence in the decision-making processes. Relationship management is the fourth episode centred on balancing independence and involvement. Executing these practices implies risk practitioners gaining referent and expert power, applying participatory, visionary, and affiliated leadership styles, identifying stakeholder needs, and recognising organisational knowledge barriers.

Keywords: risk management, effectiveness, communication, leadership, risk practitioners, ERM, Germany

1. Introduction

Managing risks is essential for organisations to survive and, thus, part of everyday business activities. Traditionally, business managers were responsible for managing risks individually on a decentralised basis [1]. Enterprise Risk Management (ERM) takes a broader perspective. To inform strategic decision-making, ERM integrates all company risks into a coordinated framework [2].

An online survey conducted by the thought leader *NC State ERM Initiative* shows that the number of companies with a complete, formal ERM increased from a single-digit percentage in 2009 to 35 per cent in 2020 [3]. However, the same survey shows that only 28 per cent of respondents consider their risk management mature or robust, and only one-third perceive their approach to risk management as valuable for strategic decision-making.

Consequently, in a survey of financial firms conducted by Deloitte [4], two-thirds of respondents consider the infusion of risk management into strategy and better cooperation between risk management and business units as having high priority. Business units must accept and support the ERM unit and processes to achieve these objectives. However, Deloitte identified these specific aspects as a critical challenge. Similarly, KPMG [5] determined in a study of non-financial firms that context-rich discussions between the ERM unit and business leaders, particularly engaging top management, remain persistent obstacles.

Overcoming these challenges is essential for effective ERM. Risk communication, creating risk awareness and culture, and gaining commitment from top management are the critical success factors when integrating ERM into decision-making processes [6]. According to Maitlis [7], increasing the acceptance of ERM units is achieved by constructing and promoting understanding by decision-makers. The extent to which risk practitioners play a leadership role in business activities and how they communicate is therefore decisive for ERM effectiveness.

This relationship is reflected in competency frameworks increasingly emphasising the relevance of risk practitioners' communication and leadership skills. Oliver Wyman [8] recognises that the ability to influence people in risk culture and top-level strategic decision-making is becoming a core competency for risk practitioners. The Institute of Risk Management (IRM), a professional body for risk management, similarly emphasises risk professionals' influence, collaboration, and relationship management capabilities [9].

Apart from a few case studies describing risk practitioners' communication practices in a company-specific context [10–13], little is known about how ERM practitioners use communication and leadership to overcome the stated challenges. In response to these gaps in the literature, this research aims to explore risk practitioners' practices to achieve ERM effectiveness, notably communication and leadership practices. It poses the following question: *What are effective communication and leadership practices of risk practitioners to achieve and maintain the effectiveness of organisational ERM?*

The notion that ERM effectiveness is achievable and maintainable acknowledges that risk is a perception influenced by the social and physical environment [14]. Organisations construct and continually reconstruct the meaning of their environment [15]. This sensemaking process is influenced by risk practitioners, who are themselves sensemakers ongoingly affecting sensemaking as members of the organisation [14]. Organisational sensemaking imposes challenges on risk practitioners that they can overcome through leadership and communication.

The research is delimited to Germany to essentially factor out multiple country-specific risk management regulations and socio-cultural variations. It contributes to an enhanced understanding of the means available for risk practitioners to increase ERM effectiveness. Further, the study extends the literature on critical success factors for risk practitioners' communication and leadership practices.

The remainder of this chapter is organised into five sections. The following section discusses the relevant literature, drawing on risk management studies and wider managerial research. The third section describes the research methods. Results are presented in the fourth section and discussed using theoretical frameworks in the fifth section. The final section concludes this research.

2. Literature

Academics disagree on the concrete constituents of ERM [16–18]. Consequently, its implementations vary substantially among companies [10, 19]. Considering ERM as a portfolio approach aiming to manage all critical risks holistically across

DOI: http://dx.doi.org/10.5772/intechopen.107066

the company and as an organisational function that creates competitive advantage is an emerging consensus [16]. However, developing resilience in the company's core competencies and seizing opportunities requires synchronising ERM with the firm's dynamic capabilities [20]. Therefore, ERM embodies change management requiring close cooperation between risk managers and business departments [21, 22].

A system's effectiveness requires incorporating the aspiration of the decision taker, who has authority and responsibility for the system and a primary concern for its performance [23, 24]. Therefore, ERM effectiveness depends on the formal power of the company's management and the informal power of the ERM unit. To gain this aspiration, ERM must support risk-informed or risk-based decisions in a disciplined way throughout the organisation [25]. Therefore, risk practitioners must understand what their stakeholders value [26]. Quantitative studies on ERM and firm performance identify risk committees as pivotal stakeholders [27–29]. Beasley et al. [30] identified the CEO and CFO as essential stakeholders who determine the success of ERM implementation.

Consequently, the quality of upward communication and leadership by risk professionals with committees, board members, and other management levels affect ERM effectiveness. However, communication and leadership are essential across the company to gain stakeholders' input to risk management processes and their ownership of outputs [22]. Accordingly, COSO [31] further identifies the business units' operational management and employees as important stakeholders.

In Germany, risk practitioners predominantly take an independent facilitator role in their companies [32]. According to Kaplan and Mikes [11], in this role, they avoid influencing formal decision-making but set agendas for highly interactive risk management discussions and facilitate risk communication up, down, and across the organisation. The authors conclude that independent facilitators contribute to ERM effectiveness as these roles reduce individual and group bias and, thus, enable more objective decisions. However, the lack of formal authority constitutes a challenge as it impedes risk practitioners from effectively challenging front-line staff [33].

2.1 Communication

Organisational activities are based on interpretation and influenced by the characteristics of the environment [34]. How decision-makers understand risk information is, therefore, subject to how they make sense of it. Daft and Weick [34] term the cognitive process sensemaking. It can be described as the 'reciprocal interaction of information seeking, meaning, ascription, and action' ([35], p. 240).

The holistic ERM context renders the sensemaking process increasingly important. First, communication involves stakeholders from different business disciplines and diverse perspectives, objectives, and backgrounds [36]. Therefore, to go beyond gathering evidence, risk practitioners must incorporate subjective knowledge to create meaning of cues [12, 14, 26] and use boundary objects to manage knowledge across boundaries [22, 37, 38].

Second, risk is a social construction resulting from perceptions influenced by the social and physical environment and prior experience and knowledge [14]. Humans tend to use judgemental heuristics and ignore or discount essential information when thinking about risk [39]. Therefore, risk perceptions are highly resistant to information [40]. Additionally, organisational barriers and biases prevent information from being considered in decision-making [11]. Therefore, risk-related decisions increasingly rely on sensemaking [14].

Sensemaking depends on the activity of a pool of diverse actors addressing a range of organisational issues [7]. Risk experts can guide the sensemaking process of decision-makers by sense giving, that is, influencing their sensemaking and meaning construction to redefine the organisational reality [41]. Using concepts of issue selling and knowledge management, Meidell and Kaarbøe [12] showed that sensegiving increases risk practitioners' influences during ERM implementation and development. Issue selling is the behaviour targeted at gaining others' attention to acknowledge and understand issues [42]. Involving the upper level, peers and others from the organisation and presenting issues evidence-based, logically, and coherently supports getting buy-in [43].

Managing knowledge across knowledge domains is key to effectively cooperating with business units. Risk experts produce knowledge by analysing gathered data and information [26]. Interdepartmentally transferring and integrating this knowledge exposes challenges. Depending on novelty and power positions, managing knowledge across boundaries requires creating common knowledge, interacting cross-functional, and exploring and exploiting boundary objects [44]. Therefore, risk professionals manage knowledge within the organisation using shared language [19, 21, 22, 45], risk talks [11, 13, 45], and developing and introducing risk management tools [11–13, 37, 46].

2.2 Leadership

Business executives consider risk management effectiveness as a leadership issue [47]. Leadership, the ability to influence, motivate, and enable others [48], is independent of formal titles or positions [49]. A participative leadership style based on openness towards ideas, new concepts, or novel products contributes to ERM effectiveness [50]. This leadership style emphasises collaboration and communication and works best for creating consensus and gaining input from others [51].

However, establishing a sound risk culture also requires creating a positive climate and applying a forward-looking and anticipatory practice [14]. To gain acceptance and appreciation, risk professionals must build relationships with business managers and executives [13] and understand their objectives and needs. Therefore, risk practitioners must likewise apply visionary and affiliated leadership styles, which involve developing and articulating a vision and building emotional bonds within the organisation [51].

The ability to influence organisational activities and decisions depends on available power sources. Position power is derived from legitimate authority [52]. It is affected by risk governance frameworks, such as the widely accepted Three Lines of Defence (3LoD) model. Davies and Zhivitskaya [33] criticise the model-inherent imbalance of power distribution. The Lehman Brothers bankruptcy exemplified that the dominance of business units in decision-making reduces risk management effectiveness [53].

The ERM unit's position power results from controlling the main information flow within the risk reporting system [54], pre-approval decision authority [55, 56], regulatory requirements [36], quality and credibility of their insights in strategic discussions [36], or design, control and use of risk tools [46].

Independent of the position, risk practitioners can develop personal power, particularly expert and referent power. Expert power facilitates risk talks [11, 13, 45]. It is gained through providing evidence and explaining reasons for requests or proposals, clear and confident communication, and listening thoughtfully to other persons' concerns and suggestions [52]. Therefore, practitioners must use a common language [21, 45] with a standard accepted vocabulary [22].

Referent power is increased by demonstrating trust and respect to others and showing concern for the needs and feelings of others and can be excised by role modelling [52]. Accordingly, Kaplan and Mikes [11] conclude that risk practitioners need strong interpersonal and communication skills to stimulate broad and wide-ranging discussions that result in qualitative and subjective risk assessments.

3. Methodology

The research aimed at advancing a fundamental understanding of risk practitioners' communication and leadership practices as means of achieving and maintaining ERM effectiveness. The qualitative study uses a cross-sectional qualitative field design. It allows understanding of risk practitioners' perceptions and connecting them to the organisational context and enables an interpretation from different perspectives.

3.1 Data collection

The research was limited to Germany to avoid influences from socio-cultural differences or country-specific risk management regulations. Participants have been recruited by a combination of self-selection and snowball sampling within the researcher's professional network. The selection included various industries and was limited to ERM leadership or senior-level positions. Instead of job titles, the classification followed IRM's career levels [9] and, thus, based on the breadth and depth of influence over stakeholders and the risk profession (**Table 1**).

Primary data have been collected through one-to-one semi-structured interviews to facilitate rich and in-depth accounts. Initial questions were shared with the interviewees before the interview to enable participants to mull over the questions and provide deeper accounts. The interviews' flow was flexible and contingent on what participants were saying. Accordingly, the formulation of questions and their order varied among interviews. Emphasis was put on how participants frame and understand issues and what an interviewee considers meaningful in ERM communication and leadership. This focus enabled explaining and understanding events, patterns,

Interviewee	Industry	Interview mode	Career level	Risk experience
1	Energy	Face-to-face	Senior	9 years
2	Chemistry	Video	Leadership	8 years
3	Food	Video	Leadership	10 years
4	Energy	Telephone	Leadership	12 years
5	Pharma	Video	Leadership	17 years
6	Manufacturing	Telephone	Leadership	9 years
7	Energy	Telephone	Senior	7 years

Table 1.
Participants of the research study.

and behaviours. The interview language concurred with the researcher's first language and the study's location.

3.2 Data analysis

The research followed an inductive approach to theory development. Instead of pre-specifying hypotheses, findings have been generated from data. Interviews have been transcribed and analysed in the source language to keep ties between language, identity, and culture as long as possible. For quotations, the material has been directly translated into the English language to achieve credibility and authenticity.

Qualitative research data have been triangulated with qualitative studies and surveys to ensure credibility. Surveys have been consulted to identify risk practitioners' challenges, contextualise risk practitioners' roles in German companies, and understand practitioners' perceptions of the present risk culture. Thick descriptions of the research findings and interpretations ensure transferability. The researcher kept complete records through all phases of the research process, including data analysis decisions and a reflective research diary to ensure dependability. Including rich quotes from participants depicting how themes have emerged ensures conformability.

The coding of interviews followed a template analysis approach in which the hierarchical representation of themes and codes emerged during the coding process. Existing literature, particularly sensemaking literature, guided the development of codes.

The coding was performed in two cycles using NVivo software. Initial coding provided breaking down data into discrete parts and determining the topic of each passage of the semi-structured interviews. Risk practitioners' challenges and actions have been identified using value coding, respectively, process coding.

In a second coding cycle, initial codes have been grouped and summarised to create smaller categories based on emergent configuration and explanation. This process included reanalysing first cycle codes, merging similar codes, and reassessing the utility of infrequent codes for the overall coding scheme.

4. Results

A salient challenge for risk practitioners is the reluctance of business units to accept new ERM initiatives or deeply involve the ERM unit in decision-making. Practitioners consider the recurrent misperception of ERM as an administrative burden pivotal for this change resistance. Additionally, individual and organisational bias, including understating risks not yet encountered by the organisation, backs misperception. Organisational knowledge domains aggravate the correction of business units' appreciation of ERM.

Regarding the company's top management, risk practitioners realise challenges through insufficient management commitment to ERM. Consequently, the ERM unit is insufficiently involved in the strategic decision-making process. Top management representatives' political and social concerns related to risk documentation and perception of their authority further undermine the ERM's strategic relevance. Risk practitioners apply practices substantiating in four episodes to overcome these challenges. **Table 2** summarises the findings, including the number of participants who mentioned the specific practice.

Praxis episodes	Practices	Description
Creating shared understanding	Understand the business (5)	Understand the requirements, objectives and operating principles of business units
	Qualify stakeholders (4)	Perform interactive training and interdisciplinary workshops with business units and management
	Visualise risk methods (3)	Explain risk knowledge through scenarios, examples, visualisation and simplification
Emphasising value creation	Strengthen transparency (6)	Reduce bias and groupthink by coordinating views and exploring consensus among the organisation
	Leveraging information (5)	Combining perspectives, using risk tools, and experimenting with ways to present information effectively
	Enhance perspectives (4)	Adding insights by exploring consequences from different perspectives
Exerting leadership practices	Strengthen influence (5)	Using power, knowledge and assertive communication and actively network
	Cultivate dialogue (5)	Establish dialogue and exchange of information. Apply appropriate language when necessary
	Foster direction (4)	Encourage decisions by incorporating objectives, adapting approaches and presenting in the language of business
	Manage tensions (4)	Solving conflicts and achieving compromises by a participatory leadership style
Managing relationships	Building trust (6)	Allow unbiased and trustful discussions. Respect and utilise competencies and responsibilities of business units
	Business partnering (6)	Consult business units on risk questions considering their interests. Create win-wins and proactively provide support
	Building relationships (4)	Establish connections with business units and actively engage in networking

Table 2.
Practice episodes and practices applied by risk practitioners.

4.1 Creating shared understanding

The first practice episode concerns creating a shared understanding between the ERM and business units. Risk practitioners develop profound and comprehensive business knowledge to enable effective risk identification, making sense of received information, and aligning the ERM system with business requirements and objectives. One interviewee summarised: 'You must have seen the way things work to understand how risks arise, to discern how to report risks effectively, and implement the risk management processes to work properly'.

Reciprocally, practitioners qualify stakeholders and create risk awareness through interdisciplinary workshops, informal dialogues and interactive training sessions to surmount boundaries of knowledge domains. They use purposeful presentation and shared language to transfer risk knowledge effectively.

Practitioners capitalise on simplification and contextualise risk theory using psychological research. Additionally, they offer examples of risk management failures in the company's business environment: 'We conduct workshops that include some fun–examples from Kahneman and Tversky, or Ralf Dobelli–and classic thinking mistakes concerning our industry. These examples support that people better understand what risk management is about and what traditional mistakes can happen. These topics increase the dialogue'.

4.2 Emphasising value creation

The second practice episode aims at creating business value. Risk practitioners holistically emphasise aspects from a company's point of view. They prioritise risks with high importance on the company level while leaving the analysis of more local risks on the business unit's level. Besides effective resource use, this prioritisation acknowledges business domain expertise and esteems cooperation. In this vein, risk practitioners consciously decide about the amount and content of information presented to avoid communication overloads: 'I would always minimise or reduce communication to the essentials. This means I only communicate as much as necessary to avoid overwhelming others with all the details'.

Participants leverage information by combining risks and business objectives, such as profitability or strategic relevance. They consciously capitalise on the advantage of a central unit for rendering interrelations between the company's risks. By experimenting with visual representations for presenting intricate risk knowledge, risk practitioners continuously optimise communication across business units and with management. They constantly create and reconfigure risk tools to further increase the sophistication of risk analysis and decisions. Risk practitioners utilise these tools to increase the effectiveness of risk communication with business units.

Furthermore, risk practitioners campaign risk discussions with business units to enhance company-wide risk perspectives. With these discussions, they anticipate potential conflicts of interest and try to find commonalities and differences in business units' perspectives on risk. While practitioners aim at joint organisational perspectives, they appreciate different perspectives to holistically inform decisions and reduce bias and groupthink in the decision-making process.

4.3 Exerting leadership practices

Exerting leadership practices represent the respondents' third practice episode. Interviewees reinforce their influence in decision-making through deliberate networking and demonstrating expertise. For this purpose, they use assertive communication and openly and confidentially express opinions: 'When I talk about risks with the Board of Management, I express my own opinion, for instance, by telling my suggestion. In this way, the board recognises me as a competent advisor'.

Risk practitioners cultivate dialogue with business units by establishing and encouraging conversations. These dialogues are encouraged by offering the ERM unit's availability for talks beyond official meetings and by assuring confidential treatment of information on request. To reinforce direction in decision-making, interviewees focus on how they present information. These considerations include describing information in the language of business units, outlying available decision options and incorporating business objectives.

Risk practitioners apply a cooperative communication style to avoid or manage tensions and ensure trustworthy cooperation with business units. In the same vein, they use ownership over information, such as risk reporting, carefully and only as the last resource to uphold trust and maintain a cooperative relationship with business units. One interviewee exemplified this: 'You have to work with people because you cannot achieve anything when working against them'. However, risk practitioners defend positions and resist undue requests from business units to champion sound risk management approaches: 'I try to be as flexible as possible in the communication with business units. However, certain things must not be adjusted'.

4.4 Managing relationships

Risk practitioners' relationship management practices aim to overcome change resistance by building trust, networking and partnering with the business. Being transparent about the ERM unit's assumptions and the intended use of received data is a routine practice. Respondents demonstrate a level playing field to distract fears that they could use information against business units. For this reason, they use factual and objective communication to build trust and avoid early judgements.

Participants emphasised the importance of partnering with the business to overcome change resistance and misperception of the ERM. Therefore, they proactively support business units in solving risk-related problems. Participants also create win-wins with other business departments through purposeful cooperation and deliberately avoid making the impression of box-ticking. As a result, they counter the perception of ERM as a valueless administrative burden: 'When you are seen as a consultant and offer solutions to specific issues, then you win the people'.

Establishing connections with business units through informal meetings and talks and active networking is a regular practice. Participants strive to develop casual relationships to overcome change resistance and reduce conflicting interests: 'You try staying in contact and up to date by knowing what is going on in the department'.

5. Discussion

Risk communication is essential to gain stakeholders' input on the risk management process and their ownership of the output [22]. Accordingly, the findings show that risk practitioners' communication and leadership practices are directed both towards business units and top management. ERM practitioners encourage and support communication about risks within the organisation without formally influencing decision-making [11]. As a result, business units can easily prevent or restrict risk practitioners' involvement in decision-making [57]. Therefore, risk practitioners emphasise creating value and building common ground for risk work, which they achieve through leadership practices and relationship management.

5.1 Gaining and using power

Risk practitioners emphasise unbiased discussions and respect other business units' competencies. This trust-building practice effectively addresses change resistance as it reframes change requests as less threatening [58]. Practitioners further reinforce trust-building by fostering dialogue with business units and management and building relationships through networking and connections.

These practices, aimed at building informal networks and increasing dialogue, overlap with the findings of studies conducted by Mikes and colleagues, as outlined in Kaplan and Mikes [11]. According to the authors, informal networks with executives and business managers help maintain a balance between keeping a sufficient distance to remain independent and staying involved in the business. The challenges mentioned by respondents elucidate this requirement. On the one hand, the ERM unit is perceived as an administrative burden responsible for controlling compliance with little relevance for decision-making. On the other hand, conflicting interests and change resistance by business units hinder the effective sharing of information.

Yukl [52] emphasises collaboration and communication as related to referent power. As the author states, this power source is an essential source of influence as people are more likely to carry out requests from persons they admire. Therefore, referent power positively affects risk practitioners' leadership practices, such as managing tensions and strengthening influence. Using their referent power, established informal networks allow risk practitioners to reshape and improve how the ERM role is perceived by executives and business units [13]. Risk practitioners must develop a consistent set of values, clearly express them and act based on them to increase referent power [52].

Risk practitioners strengthen their influence using two additional power sources. The first is expert power, a personal power source. Yukl [52] confirms unique knowledge as a potential source for influencing subordinates, peers and superiors. Moreover, as influence is more likely to be accepted and less rejected when exercised by people with critical and scarce knowledge, expert power is superior to participative leadership [59]. Expert power allows risk practitioners to share opinions proactively and openly and, thus, be recognised as competent advisors for the management. Risk practitioners must present rational arguments appreciatively and humbly to gain and maintain expert power [52]. To be recognised by decision-makers as experts require building informal networks and proactively providing expert opinions from a risk perspective.

As a second power source to strengthen their influence, risk practitioners possess information power, a position power source. Despite having no formal authority as independent facilitators, the risk unit presents risk information to the top management. Control over information enables risk practitioners to influence risk management activities within the organisation [52]. However, position power is lost with the position associated with the power [60]. Therefore, risk practitioners reluctantly use power over information. This parallels the limited use of legitimate power found by Mikes [13] in two case studies.

Risk practitioners must manage tensions as a result of different interests. They overcome these tensions using participative leadership. Participation and collaboration enable sharing perspectives [51]. Furthermore, it increases the speed at which threats and opportunities can be identified and addressed [50]. In contrast, compromising can be counterproductive as harmony is prioritised over value [61]. For risk practitioners, this implies prioritising negotiation of claims over compromise-seeking strategies.

5.2 Increasing influence through issue selling

Issue selling is centred on affecting others' attention. The framework developed by Dutton and Ashford [42] and Dutton et al. [43] considers how middle managers gain influence through issue selling in upward communication. Still, the observation of Dutton et al. [43] observation that issue selling is a political and commitment-building process parallels the process through which risk practitioners engage with peers.

When risk practitioners emphasise value creation, such as leveraging information and enhancing perspectives, they predominantly use logical, coherent, structured presentations and incorporate business objectives. These practices create legitimacy on issues to be sold and increase attention by decision-makers [43].

According to Dutton et al. [43], bundling risk issues with business objectives is successful if these issues are linked to already agreed-upon goals. Risk practitioners must identify stakeholders, practice relationship building and develop knowledge about the organisation's strategy. The authors note that issue-selling efforts should be customised to include the full range of stakeholders. Beyond knowing stakeholders, customisation may involve experimenting with alternatives to present knowledge, as one interviewee specified.

Practices aiming to develop this knowledge include fostering dialogue and building trust. These practices involve the informal exchange of information and emphasise unbiased and trustful discussions. Involving others helps reduce bias through diverse thoughts [62]. It further increases visibility, creates awareness and supports building organisational commitment [43]. Practitioners reinforce involvement through a participatory leadership style that builds trust, respect and commitment [51]. Therefore, these practices help increase risk practitioners' influence and overcome change resistance.

In the same vein, involvement helps to reduce the misperception of ERM and reinforces relation-building practices. However, as Goleman [51] flags, participation must be distinguished from putting off crucial decisions, confusing people and escalating conflicts. As the findings show, it implies that risk practitioners communicate assertively, including resisting conflicting demands. Assertive communication emphasises expressing opinions and beliefs honestly and appropriately without infringing on others' emotions [63]. Therefore, assertively resisting conflicting demands helps keeping a balance between independence and involvement [13].

5.3 Managing knowledge across boundaries

Creating a shared understanding and value for the business are two major practice episodes pursued by risk practitioners. Through these episodes, they understand the business, including objectives and requirements. It also involves transferring knowledge on ERM to stakeholders. These practices help risk practitioners and business units create common knowledge. Common knowledge is necessary for sharing and assessing knowledge across boundaries [44]. Using this knowledge and, particularly, applying the language of the business reinforce risk practitioners' leadership practices, such as cultivating dialogue.

Risk practitioners increase interaction with business units by developing and applying business language in conversations [12, 13, 46]. Carlile [44] states that a common lexicon is sufficient for managing dependencies between activities and resources where knowledge differences and dependencies between actors are known.

Increasing novelty blurs differences and dependencies and makes meanings ambiguous [44]. Therefore, risk practitioners visualise risk methods using scenarios, examples and simplification. Moreover, they use their risk tools to leverage information. Risk tools can effectively represent and transform current and novel knowledge [46], thus supporting the interaction between risk practitioners and others.

When novelty leads to conflicting interests, it impedes effectively sharing information and knowledge [44]. Overlapping activities resulting from shared accountability for managing uncertainties stimulate professional rivalry [10] and reinforce conflicting interests. These conflicts require creating common meanings and renegotiating agreements [44]. The participative leadership style used by risk practitioners supports this objective [61]. Therefore, participation effectively overcomes knowledge boundaries, especially in volatile business environments characterised by high novelty.

Risk practitioners complement collaboration by partnering with business units to create win-wins and reframe the organisational ERM. According to Carlile and Rebentisch [64], reframing the perception of ERM as a value-creating practice fosters cooperation through the demand for value-creating activities. However, a high level of novelty generates different interests [44] expressed by political and social concerns. According to Carlile [44], interests must be negotiated and defined in a political process. As the author states, costs resulting from transforming current common and domain-specific knowledge negatively impact the willingness of actors to make those changes. Therefore, partnering with business units enables risk practitioners to discuss and stipulate shared interests.

Risk practitioners require stakeholders' input to risk management processes [22]. However, individual biases and groupthink jeopardise the quality of shared information and, thus, the quality of consequent decisions [65]. These issues promote overlooking threats or subjective assessments [11]. Risk practitioners acknowledge different perspectives from diverse stakeholders and incorporate them into their knowledge generation to overcome individual bias and combat groupthink. This diversity of thoughts is essential for effective decision-making as it supports understanding the full range of possible options [62].

6. Conclusion

While many companies implement ERM to inform strategic decision-making, most struggle with its effectiveness. This research explores risk practitioners' communication and leadership practices to achieve and maintain ERM effectiveness. Findings result from data collected through semi-structured interviews among leadership and senior-level ERM practitioners across various industries.

The study identifies four practice episodes. First, risk practitioners create shared knowledge between business units and the ERM unit. Practitioners fathom business concerns, requirements and objectives, and reciprocally qualify stakeholders and create risk awareness. Second, practitioners demonstrate the value-creating capabilities of ERM. They capitalise on the high-level perspective of a central ERM unit to leverage data and information through contextualisation. Practitioners acknowledge business domain expertise and esteem cooperation by dividing and prioritising risk work based on value-adding capabilities.

Third, practitioners consciously exert leadership practices to strengthen their influence in decision-making and champion sound risk management. They use participation to emphasise trust and get the buy-in of stakeholders. Using assertiveness, they withstand undue requests and advocate sound risk management standards.

Leadership practices affect relationship building, the fourth practice episode. Practitioners network to overcome organisational change resistance and balance independence and involvement. They are partnering with and proactively supporting business units in risk aspects to reframe ERM and avoid tensions.

The study forms a practical guide for risk practitioners to manage ERM effectiveness. Applying these practices requires practitioners to develop and emphasise referent and expert power. Practitioners must identify stakeholders and understand their needs to sell issues and effectively encourage decisions. Practitioners must continuously develop a common language for effectively transferring knowledge within the organisation, understand when knowledge boundaries blur and constantly explore and exploit boundary objects. For organisations, the research provides opportunities for shareholder value creation by optimising risk practitioner development programs and setting the course for higher ERM effectiveness.

The research is limited to Germany to ensure an unambiguous socio-cultural and country-specific setting. The narrow scope constitutes a limitation, and future in-depth case studies are required to understand how cultural and intercultural aspects influence risk practitioners' ERM practices.

Acknowledgements

I thank Christian Dommers (Deloitte GmbH) for providing access to Deloitte's network of ERM practitioners. This extension of my professional network substantially supported selecting ERM practitioners in senior and leadership positions from various industries.

Author details

Thomas Wolter
Independent Scientist, Berlin, Germany

*Address all correspondence to: thwolter@gmail.com

References

[1] Beasley MS. What is Enterprise Risk Management? NC State: Poole College of Management; 2016. Available from: https://erm.ncsu.edu/az/erm/i/chan/library/What_is_Enterprise_Risk_Management.pdf. [Accessed: 23 May 2020]

[2] Schiller F, Prpich G. Learning to organise risk management in organisations: What future for enterprise risk management? Journal of Risk Research. 2014;**17**(8):999-1017

[3] Beasley MS, Branson BC, Hancock BV. The State of Risk Oversight. NC State: Poole College of Management; 2021. Available from: https://erm.ncsu.edu/az/erm/i/chan/library/2021-risk-oversight-report-erm-ncstate.pdf. [Accessed: 16 June 2022]

[4] Deloitte. Global Risk Management Survey. 11th ed. Deloitte; 2018. Available from: https://www2.deloitte.com/bg/en/pages/finance/articles/global-risk-management-survey-2019.html. [Accessed: 7 June 2020]

[5] KPMG. Enterprise Risk Management Benchmarking Study. KPMG. Available from: https://advisory.kpmg.us/content/dam/advisory/en/pdfs/erm-benchmarking-brochure.pdf; 2019. [Accessed: 6 June 2020]

[6] Oliveira K, Méxas M, Meiriño M, Drumond G. Critical success factors associated with the implementation of enterprise risk management. Journal of Risk Research. 2019;**22**(8):1004-1019

[7] Maitlis S. The social processes of organisational sensemaking. Academy of Management Journal. 2005;**48**(1):21-49

[8] Oliver Wyman. Risk Leadership - Changing the Pardigm. Oliver Wyman; 2017. Available from: https://www.oliverwyman.com/content/dam/oliver-wyman/v2/publications/2017/sep/RISK_LEADERSHIP_2017.pdf. [Accessed: 22 June 2020]

[9] IRM. Professional Standards in Risk Management. IRM. Available from: https://www.theirm.org/what-we-do/about-us/professional-standards/. [Accessed: 6 June 2020]

[10] Arena M, Arnaboldi M, Azzone G. The organisational dynamics of enterprise risk management. Accounting, Organisations and Society. 2010;**35**(7):659-675

[11] Kaplan RS, Mikes A. Risk management-the revealing hand, journal of applied corporate. Finance. 2016;**28**(1):8-18

[12] Meidell A, Kaarbøe K. How the enterprise risk management function influences decision-making in the organisation – A field study of a large, global oil and gas company. British Accounting Review. 2017;**49**(1):39-55

[13] Mikes A. The triumph of the humble chief risk officer. In: Power M, editor. Riskwork: Essays on the Organisational Life of Risk Management. Oxford, UK: Oxford University Press; 2016. pp. 253-273

[14] Taarup-Esbensen J. Making sense of risk—A sociological perspective on the management of risk. Risk Analysis. 2019;**39**(4):749-760

[15] Weick KE. Sensemaking in Organisations. London, UK: Sage; 1995

[16] Bromiley P, McShane M, Nair A, Rustambekov E. Enterprise

risk management: Review, critique, and research directions. Long Range Planning. 2015;**48**(4):265-276

[17] Perera AAS. Enterprise risk management–international standards and frameworks. International Journal of Scientific and Research Publications. 2019;**9**(7):211-217

[18] Rochette M. From risk management to ERM. Journal of Risk Management in Financial Institutions. 2009;**2**(4):394-408

[19] Mikes A. Risk management and calculative cultures. Management Accounting Research. 2009;**20**(1): 18-40

[20] Bogodistov Y, Wohlgemuth V. Enterprise risk management: A capability-based perspective. The Journal of Risk Finance. 2017;**18**(3):234-251

[21] Fraser JR, Simkins BJ. The challenges of and solutions for implementing enterprise risk management. Business Horizons. 2016;**59**(6):689-698

[22] McShane M. Enterprise risk management: History and a design science proposal. The Journal of Risk Finance. 2018;**19**(2):137-153

[23] Checkland P. Soft systems methodology: A thirty year retrospective. Systems Research and Behavioral Science. 2000;**17**(S1):S11-S58

[24] Bergvall-Kåreborn B, Mirijamdotter A, Basden A. Basic principles of SSM modeling: An examination of CATWOE from a soft perspective. Systemic Practice and Action Research. 2004;**17**(2):55-73

[25] Brooks DW. Creating a risk-aware culture. In: Fraser J, Simkins BJ, editors. Enterprise Risk Management. New York: Wiley & Sons; 2010. pp. 87-95

[26] Aven T. Risk assessment and risk management: Review of recent advances on their foundation. European Journal of Operational Research. 2016;**253**(1):1-13

[27] Florio C, Leoni G. Enterprise risk management and firm performance: The Italian case. The British Accounting Review. 2017;**49**(1):56-74

[28] Gordon LA, Loeb MP, Tseng C-Y. Enterprise risk management and firm performance: A contingency perspective. Journal of Accounting and Public Policy. 2009;**28**(4):301-327

[29] Malik MF, Zaman M, Buckby S. Enterprise risk management and firm performance: Role of the risk committee. Journal of Contemporary Accounting & Economics. 2020;**16**(1):100178

[30] Beasley MS, Clune R, Hermanson DR. Enterprise risk management: An empirical analysis of factors associated with the extent of implementation. Journal of Accounting and Public Policy. 2005;**24**(6):521-531

[31] COSO. Applying Enterprise Risk Management to Environmental, Social and Governance-Related Risks. COSO; 2018. Available from: https://www.wbcsd.org/Programs/Redefining-Value/Business-Decision-Making/Enterprise-Risk-Management/Resources/Applying-Enterprise-Risk-Management-to-Environmental-Social-and-Governance-related-Risks. [Accessed: 28 July 2020]

[32] Deloitte, Benchmarkstudie Risikomanagement, Deloitte, 2020. Available from: https://www2.deloitte.com/de/de/pages/audit/articles/risikomanagement-benchmarkstudie-2020.html. [Accessed: 16 July 2020]

[33] Davies H, Zhivitskaya M. Three lines of defence: A robust organising

framework, or just lines in the sand? Global Policy. 2018;**9**:34-42

[34] Daft RL, Weick KE. Toward a model of organisations as interpretation systems. Academy of Management Review. 1984;**9**(2):284-295

[35] Thomas JB, Clark SM, Gioia DA. Strategic sensemaking and organisational performance: Linkages among scanning, interpretation, action, and outcomes. Academy of Management Journal. 1993;**36**(2):239-270

[36] Mikes A. Chief risk officers at crunch time: Compliance champions or business partners? Journal of Risk Management in Financial Institutions. 2008;**2**(1);7-25

[37] Jordan S, Jørgensen L, Mitterhofer H. Performing risk and the project: Risk maps as mediating instruments. Management Accounting Research. 2013;**24**(2):156-174

[38] Romme AGL, Damen IC. Toward science-based design in organisation development: Codifying the process. The Journal of Applied Behavioral Science. 2007;**43**(1):108-121

[39] Kahneman D, Lovallo D, Sibony O. Before you make that big decision. Harvard Business Review. 2011;**89**(6):50-60

[40] Arvai J. The end of risk communication as we know it. Journal of Risk Research. 2014;**17**(10):1245-1249

[41] Gioia DA, Chittipeddi K. Sensemaking and sensegiving in strategic change initiation. Strategic Management Journal. 1991;**12**(6):433-448

[42] Dutton JE, Ashford SJ. Selling issues to top management. Academy of Management Review. 1993;**18**(3):397-428

[43] Dutton JE, Ashford SJ, O'Neill RM, Lawrence KA. Moves that matter: Issue selling and organisational change. Academy of Management Journal. 2001;**44**(4):716-736

[44] Carlile PR. Transferring, translating, and transforming: An integrative framework for managing knowledge across boundaries. Organization Science. 2004;**15**(5):555-568

[45] Ashby S, Bryce C and Ring P. Risk and Performance: Embedding Risk Management. London, UK: Association of Chartered Certified Accountants (ACCA). 2019. Available from: http://hdl.handle.net/20.500.12127/6367. [Accessed: 5 August 2020]

[46] Hall M, Mikes A, Millo Y. How do risk managers become influential? A field study of toolmaking in two financial institutions. Management Accounting Research. 2015;**26**:3-22

[47] Campbell KA. Can effective risk management signal virtue-based leadership? Journal of Business Ethics. 2015;**129**(1):115-130

[48] House R, Javidan M, Hanges P, Dorfman P. Understanding cultures and implicit leadership theories across the globe: An introduction to project GLOBE. Journal of World Business. 2002;**37**(1):3-10

[49] Nahavandi A. The Art and Science of Leadership. Harlow, Essex, England: Pearson Education Limited; 2015

[50] Sax J, Torp SS. Speak up! Enhancing risk performance with enterprise risk management, leadership style and employee voice. Management Decision. 2015;**53**(7):1452-1468

[51] Goleman D. Leadership that gets results. Harvard Business Review. 2000;**78**(2):78-90

[52] Yukl G. Leadership in Organisations. 8th ed. Harlow, England: Pearson Education Limited; 2013

[53] Rooney J, Cuganesan S. Leadership, governance and the mitigation of risk: A case study, managerial auditing journal. Limited. 2015;**30**(2):132

[54] Giovannoni E, Quarchioni S, Riccaboni A. The role of roles in risk management change: The case of an Italian bank. European Accounting Review. 2016;**25**(1):109-129

[55] Mikes A. From counting risk to making risk count: Boundary-work in risk management. Accounting, organisations and society. 2011;**36**(4):226-245

[56] Mikes A, Kaplan RS. When one size doesn't fit all: Evolving directions in the research and practice of enterprise risk management. Journal of Applied Corporate Finance. 2015;**27**(1):37-40

[57] Stulz RM. Risk-taking and risk management by banks. Journal of Applied Corporate Finance. 2015;**27**(1):8-18

[58] Kotter JP, Schlesinger LA. Choosing strategies for change. Harvard Business Review. 2008;**86**(7/8):130-139

[59] Lines R. Using power to install strategy: The relationships between expert power, position power, influence tactics and implementation success. Journal of Change Management. 2007;**7**(2):143-170

[60] Caproni PJ. Management Skills for Everyday Life: The Practical Coach. 3rd ed. Boston: Prentice Hall; 2012

[61] Whetten DA, Cameron KS. Developing Management Skills. Global ed. Harlow, United Kingdom: Pearson; 2015

[62] Bruce JR. Risky business: How social psychology can help improve corporate risk management. Business Horizons. 2014;**57**(4):551-557

[63] Back K, Back K. Assertiveness at Work. 3rd ed. London, UK: McGraw-Hill; 2005

[64] Carlile PR, Rebentisch ES. Into the black box: The knowledge transformation cycle. Management Science. 2003;**49**(9):1180-1195

[65] Chaffey D, White G. Business Information Management: Improving Performance Using Information Systems. Harlow: Prentice Hall; 2005

Chapter 6

Risk Management Tools to Improve the Efficiency of Lending to Retail Segments

Mikhail Pomazanov

Abstract

This chapter discusses the issue of assessing the quality of risk management for a wide segment of retail lending (from consumer loans to loans for self-employed persons and SMEs). The quality of risk management is assessed using the generally recognized approach of the ROC analysis methodology and assessment of the optimal level of discrimination, taking into account risk-return. The chapter substantiates a marginal formula for assessing the economic benefits of improving the discriminatory power of the scoring models on which risk management is based. Based on the presented approach, it is possible to economically justify the costs of investment resources aimed at improving models and their technical implementation in credit business processes. An assessment of the quality of risk management in the mass lending segment reveals problems in lending strategies caused by the inefficiency of return in relation to risk in individual segments. This provides evidence-based grounds for adjusting strategies. The review of perspective modern directions of development and improvement of scoring models is presented.

Keywords: probability of default, gini index, profit, efficiency, validation, risk-management, credit, retail

1. Introduction

Modern recommendations of banking supervision reflect the requirements for the organization of the use of internal rating models and their quality, allowing the bank to bring the regulatory requirements of reserves and capital closer to economically justified, i.e., risk-sensitive [1]. The requirements of the National Banking Regulator are complex, concerning the preparation of high-quality and validated data for the development of models, the requirements for the development itself, the administrative independence of developers from the interests of business, regular validation of models on current data, systematic refinement of risk assessment models, etc. When deficiencies in discriminatory ability or stability are identified, the requirements define mandatory regular reporting to the Bank's Management and the Regulator on the results of quality analysis of the applied internal rating models. The requirements for the risk and capital management system of the banking group through the implementation of internal procedures for assessing capital adequacy reflect the requirements [2] to establish the procedure and frequency for assessing the effectiveness of risk assessment methods. It is required to update the documents that establish risk assessment methods and the procedure for validating quantitative models. Obviously, the implementation of these requirements is costly for the bank, including the participation of highly qualified specialists, and the improvement of IT infrastructure and business processes. Therefore, the question arises of the adequacy of costs in relation to the credit institution's own economic effect with an increase in the level of efficiency of risk assessment methods, as well as a management decision-making system based on these methods.

Improving the quality of risk assessment modeling brings financial and nonfinancial benefits in terms of the following points:

1. savings on losses associated with credit risk in terms of reducing potential losses by more carefully separating "bad" and "good" borrowers;

2. improving the transparency of the lending business, stimulating the improvement and optimization of the lending business process, and taking into account the risks;

3. improving the image of the credit institution in terms of audit, rating agencies, and investors;

4. meeting the requirements of the National banking regulator in ensuring risk management standards and loss provisions.

The introduction of credit scoring in the banking sector has privileges which have been summarised by Al Amari [3] as follows: more efficient processing time, and subsequent support for the decision-making process; minimization of credit process costs and effort; fewer errors made; provision of estimations to be compared in post audits; inclusion of variables supported through objective analysis to assess the credit risk; modeling based on real data; interrelation between variables are considered; fewer customer-information needs for credit decisions; the cut-off score can be changed according to environmental factors affecting the banking sector.

The direct financial benefit of the first bullet is determined by the discriminatory power of the borrower's analytics based on scoring risk assessment models. This is especially true for mass banking products.

Credit scoring has been considered a major scoring tool for the past several decades and has been widely studied in various fields, including finance and accounting. Various scoring methods are used in the fields of classification and forecasting, where statistical methods are commonly used. The literature explores both complex and traditional techniques, as well as criteria for evaluating effectiveness. In [4], it provides a comprehensive review of 214 articles/books/abstracts that relate to the applications of credit scoring in various fields in general, but primarily in finance and banking. This paper provides a broad overview of various statistical methods and performance evaluation criteria. This review [4] showed that there is no best statistical method to use when building scoring models.

To increase the power of credit scoring, in the presence of the Big Data of individuals, various methods are used, including those based on artificial intelligence methods. As shown in [5], organizations by applying deep learning and machine learning techniques can tap individuals who are not being serviced by traditional financial institutions. If systems can be designed to accommodate more pragmatic analysis conditions, then this can help improve the conditions of the client profile analysis process. At the same time, process models should be developed for comprehensive analysis and then they can become a sustainable solution for managing the loan system.

The significant dependence of the profit of lending and investing in debt instruments on the quality of risk management has been substantiated by many studies. In [6], the authors developed a model for evaluating the profit that the improvement of rating systems brings. Results of a numerical analysis indicate that improving a rating system with low accuracy to medium accuracy can increase the annual rate of return on a portfolio by 30–40 bp. Therefore, compared to the estimated implementation costs, banks could have a strong incentive to invest in their rating systems. In [7], it is shown that the simple cut-off approach can be extended to a more complete pricing approach, which is more flexible and more profitable. Demonstrated that, in general, more powerful models are more beneficial than weaker ones, provides an example of modeling, and demonstrates the benefit in absolute terms. Later work [8] also examines the economic benefits of using credit scoring models, linking the discriminatory power of the credit scoring model to the optimal credit decision.

The main idea of the presented approach is based on the fundamental analogy of risk management activities with a certain generalized rating/scoring system, which also makes decisions in the retail lending segment. Risk management can be matched to the ROC/CAP-curve, and its power of discrimination can be assessed [9]. Then, determine how optimally such a rating system makes decisions, considering its own power and exogenous risk-return factors.

Approaches to assessing economic efficiency using the ROC-curve methodology were proposed earlier, but they were not directly related to risk management in lending. In [10], the authors' study indicates that banks have incentives to voluntarily participate in a positive credit information exchange mechanism. Because even a small difference in discriminatory power arising from an information gap can lead to a significant drop in profitability since the distribution of change in borrower quality is endogenous due to adverse selection problems. A paper [11] presents a methodology for assessing the economic value of adding additional data to predictive modeling applications. The methodology is based on the representation of the ROC curve and begins with an assessment of the impact of additional data on the performance of the model in terms of overall classification scores. This effect is then translated into economic units, which give the expected economic value that the firm would receive from acquiring a particular information asset. With this valuation, the firm can then set a data acquisition price that targets a specific return on investment. In the work presented in Section 2, we will answer the question of assessing the effectiveness of risk management in making credit decisions and give a methodology for validation. Section 3 proves the formula for marginal profit when the scoring model is improved in units of the Gini index. Section 4 specifies the area in the Gini coordinates and the ratio of profit to risk, where the marginal economic effect, defined by the presented formula, takes place. Section 5 discusses practical cases that are resolved using the marginal formula and typical causes of risk management inefficiency, as well as an overview of current trends in the development of scoring modeling.

2. Method for evaluating effectiveness indicators of risk management in retail lending business

Let's simulate the situation, assuming that a fixed number of applicants applied for a loan to the bank B . At the same time, a number A of them passed the procedure of credit risk management and received a loan. We also know the number D of defaults among those who received the loan. Let's also assume that we can evaluate the situation in the credit market and know which share DR would have defaulted if it had not gone through our credit risk management procedure but would have received a loan as soon as it asked for it.

The entire population of applications can be presented in the form of **Table 1**, in which all values are given to the results of the bank's risk management procedures. The values in the lighter cells are the result of the calculation, while the values in the remaining cells are objective data.

From **Table 1**, you can see the classification errors (Type I errors, Type II errors [12]):

- Type I errors—applications were rejected, but the servicing of similar loans on the market by "refuseniks" was not accompanied by a default: $B \times (1–DR)–A + D$;
- Type II errors—a positive decision was made, but servicing the loan was accompanied by the realization of the target variable, i.e., default D.

Parameters A end D are known exactly after the choice of the period for which the effectiveness of risk management is assessed. However, the parameters B end DR require additional calculation. In [13], a method for estimating these parameters and substantiating the corresponding formulas. The parameter B (the number of applicants who applied to the bank) should be adjusted taking into account the number of borrowers who were approved, but for some reason did not take a loan. This parameter will be less than the number of personal applications that have been considered. The parameter DR is also not equivalent to the share of defaulted borrowers for the selected period, which can be obtained from the standardized credit history bureau bulletin for the lending segment of interest. Because if a client comes to the bank and is denied a loan application, then there is a probability not equal to one that this client will receive a loan from another bank. Therefore, the population of applicants coming to the bank is not equivalent to the population of borrowers receiving a loan in the market, which is monitored by the Credit Bureau, it is worse. To assess the scale of this phenomenon, a specialized report of the Credit Bureau helps to find out the share of such applicants among the "refuseniks" of the bank, as well as the quality of servicing the loans they received. This requires additional research, which is practiced, and it is quite legal.

The result of the risk management decision	Default	No default	Total
Refuse	B × DR – D	B × (1 – DR) – A + D	B – A
Loan issued	D	A – D	A
Total	B × DR	B × (1 – DR)	B

Table 1.
Segmentation of the applicant population in terms of risk management.

After evaluating the above parameters, **Table 1** will give the coordinates of the fat dot **Figure 1**.

Through this bold point, you can draw a CAP[1] curve, according to which you can evaluate the Gini index, which is a generally recognized measure of the discriminatory power of the rating system, equivalent to the work of the entire risk management (more precisely, the quasi-Gini index).

To restore the CAP curve, the well-known Van der Burgt model [14] is used, which has an independent variable k that is a solution to the equation:

$$CAP(x) = \frac{1 - e^{-kx}}{1 - e^{-k}}, \tag{1}$$

where k is a parameter showing the effectiveness (power) of risk management decisions.

The constructed curve includes a point known to us, the coordinates of which we know:

$$x = \frac{B\text{–}A}{\mathrm{B}}, CAP(x) = \frac{B \times \mathrm{DR}\text{–}D}{B \times \mathrm{DR}}$$

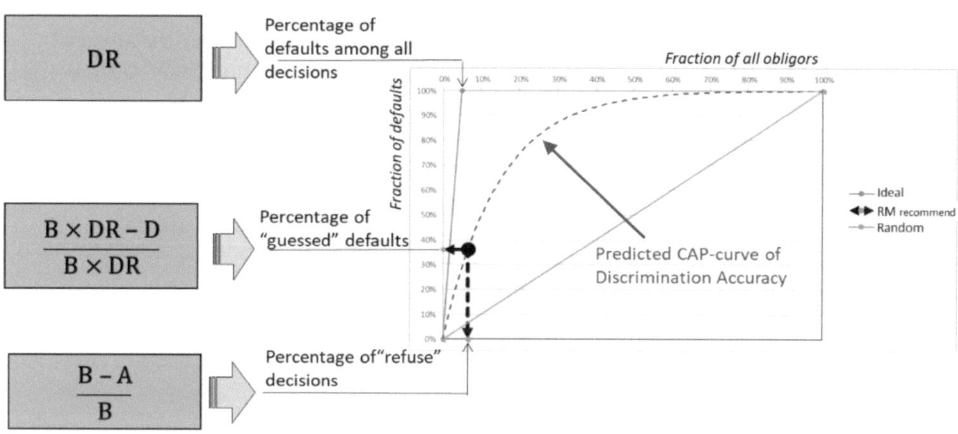

Figure 1.
Reconstruction of the CAP-curve of discriminatory accuracy of risk management procedures.

Model	Gini ranges		
	Red zone (%)	Yellow zone (%)	Green zone (%)
Behavioral	<40	40–60	>60
Applicative	<35	35–55	>55

Table 2.
Stereotypical recommendations of zonal assessments of the Gini metric.

[1] Cumulative Accuracy Profile.

The Gini curve index (1) is calculated by the formula:

$$Gini(k, DR) = \frac{2}{1 - DR} \times \left(\frac{1}{1 - e^{-k}} - \frac{1}{k} - \frac{1}{2} \right), \tag{2}$$

which sets an objective metric of the power of discriminatory risk management procedures.

Obviously, the requirements for this metric may or may not be very strict, but the widely used recommendations of zonal estimates can be offered as a baseline for retail lending banking practice (**Table 2**).

Each obtained value of the Gini index of all cumulative risk management procedures can be attributed to one or another zone. The concept of totality means that not one internal procedure, for example, a scoring model, is evaluated, but the whole set of rules and procedures is used by risk management to make a decision on a loan application. The complex uses, among other things, antifraud, manual underwriting tools, brake lights, etc.

The next tool for assessing the effectiveness of risk management should be the assessment of commercial effectiveness. To what extent is the point of "refusal" justified from the point of view of the economics of lending to the retail product under study in a bank? It is clear that the optimal discrimination point for “bad” and “good” borrowers should correspond to the level of losses EL(x) that do not exceed the marginal return (M) on the loan product.

The level of expected losses EL will be determined by the level of default of borrowers who have passed the approval procedure above the level of the quantile position x of the entire population of applicants

$$\mathrm{EL}(\mathrm{x}, \mathrm{Gini}) = \mathrm{DR} \times (1 - \mathrm{CAP}(\mathrm{x}, \ \mathrm{Gini})) \times \mathrm{LGD}. \tag{3}$$

This level is determined by Type II errors and the level of losses given default (LGD). Where CAP(x, Gini)) will be determined through the expressions (1) and (2), which are defined in the previous step of estimating the discriminating power.

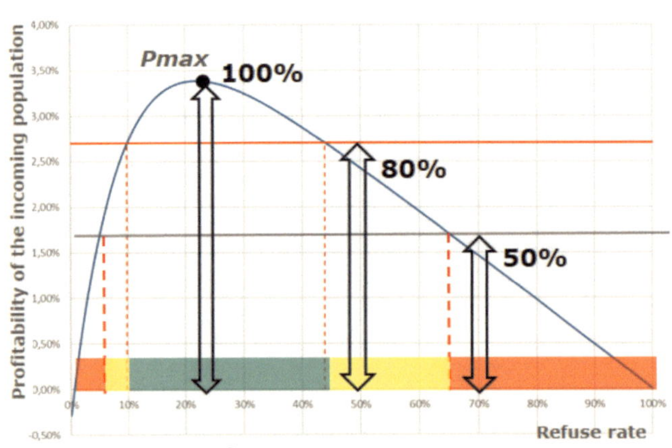

Figure 2.
Zonal representation of approval levels relative to the optimal profit level.

Assuming that the value M is given as NPV rate of the income of the credit product under study for the vintage period, taking into account all costs and terms of amortization of loans (credits), then we can propose a simple formula for the profit from a unit volume of all incoming applicants:

$$\mathrm{P(x, Gini) = M - x \times M - EL(x, Gini)} \tag{4}$$

Formula (4) simultaneously depends on Type I/II errors. Moreover, their balance is determined by external factors—the level of the market default rate and the profitability of the product. Gross profit (4) will have a maximum at a certain level of approval (optimal rejection rate) because with complete rejection, all applicants' $\mathrm{P(1, Gini) = 0}$ and vice versa, if you approve everyone, then you can have a loss if $\mathrm{DR} \times LGD > M$.

The question of determining the parameter regions where the maximum exists will be considered in the next section. But it can be argued that in the condition of equilibrium activity of the credit market (there is no excess profit and excessive demand, there is no global depression and catastrophic risks, etc.), such a maximum takes place. Therefore, it is logical to formulate the efficiency metric of commercial approval/rejection decisions in terms of the levels of deviation of these decisions from the maximum efficiency. And both in the direction of more approval, and less. **Figure 2** shows the profit curve.

Typical evaluation zones are indicated. Typical zonal levels are not the most stringent, but each bank can zone this metric for itself based on its own experience and goals.

The allowable level α of failure range $\left[X_\alpha^-, X_\alpha^+\right]$ is calculated quite simply:

- optimal failure point is calculated $\mathrm{X_{opt}} = \frac{1}{\mathrm{k}} \ln\left(\frac{\mathrm{DR \cdot LGD \cdot k}}{\mathrm{M \cdot (1 - e^{-k})}}\right)$;
- find the roots of the equation X_α^-, X_α^+: $(1-\alpha) \cdot \mathrm{P(X_{opt}, Gini(k)) = P(X_\alpha^\pm, Gini(k))}$, where $\mathrm{P(x, Gini(k))}$ follows from (2)-(4).

As a result, we get two tools for evaluating the effectiveness of risk management in a given segment of the retail lending business. The first is an assessment of the discriminating power of risk management, and the second is the economic efficiency of the credit policy, considering risks (the cut-off level).

3. Marginal economic effect improving of the discrimination power of bank borrowers

To assess the discriminating power of a rating system (model) in financial engineering, curves are traditionally used that determine its quality [15, 16], this analytics is borrowed from a well-developed theory of radio signal reception. Any rating (or scoring) system, if it confidently discriminates between "good" and "bad" borrowers, will spread the initial statistical distribution of customers by rating (scoring) score s. That is, two different distributions are obtained - default, with a density of $f_D(s)$, and nondefault, with a density of $f_N(s)$, which can be determined by the expiration of the term (usually one year) after the "measurement" of the rating s.

The probability distribution functions of getting into the rating below s for nondefault and default clients will be expressed by the corresponding integrals[2]

$$F_N(s) = \int_{-\infty}^{s} f_N(\xi)d\xi, F_D(s) = \int_{-\infty}^{s} f_D(\xi)d\xi, F_N(s) \in [0, 1], F_D(s) \in [0, 1].$$

ROC[3] end CAP curves are defined in the square of unit area on the plane (X, Y) in parametric form:

$$ROC(x) = F_D(s),\ x = F_N(s),$$
$$CAP(x) = F_D(s),\ x = (1 - p) \cdot F_N(s) + p \cdot F_D(s),$$

where $p = DR$ (likewise (3)) is the share of defaults for the period under review.

From the CAP and ROC curves, the exact formula [17] can be used to express the default probability of the borrower, whose position in the rating is determined by the coordinate $x \in [0, 1]$ (local position in the distribution of all borrowers)[4]:

$$PD(x) = p \cdot CAP'(x), \tag{5}$$

or

$$PD(x) = \frac{p \cdot ROC'(x)}{p \cdot ROC'(x) + 1 - p}, \tag{6}$$

where x—quantile position of the borrower among nondefault one. The Gini index will be calculated using the well-known formula

$$AR = \frac{2 \cdot \int_0^1 CAP(x)dx - 1}{1 - p}. \tag{7}$$

According to formulas (5) and (6), the dependence of the default probability on the rating will be largely determined by the behavior of the CAP (or ROC) curves of the rating model, as well as the distribution of borrowers (companies, clients) by rating score.

The average annual expected losses for the borrower EL are determined by the formula $\cdot LGD$, so the expected loss for a borrower with a quantile x coordinate will be determined as follows:

$$EL(x) = PD(x) \cdot LGD = p \cdot LGD \cdot CAP'(x) = EL \cdot CAP'(x), \tag{8}$$

where $EL = p \cdot LGD$ is the average market loss parameter, which is exogenous.

Suppose that the bank has an unlimited resource base and is potentially ready to lend to the entire flow of incoming applications, with a volume of "1", then it will receive a

---

[2] If the rating score or rating is not continuous (i.e., has a limited number of positions), then the integral is replaced by the sum, and the distribution over the rating is discrete.

[3] Receiver Operating Characteristic.

[4] Here and below, the prime denotes the derivative, as in the conventional notation.

loss, with a volume of EL. However, the rating system (i.e., the entire risk management process) rejects x (%) of the incoming flow, generating a loss,[5] due to unrealized profit, determined by the credit margin M. In addition, there are credit losses among system-approved borrowers (3) $EL_x = EL \cdot (1 - CAP(x))$ (**Figure 3**).

The economic effect of improving the rating system has two fundamental components. The first is the reduction in risk EL_x among approved borrowers, which is obvious since the improved rating system will have a steeper profile of the $EL(x)$ schedule, which means that the level of losses will be lower. The second is a decrease in the level of deviation (cut-off), which implies an increase in the volume of the loan portfolio with a constant flow of applicants and constant lending rates.

We introduce the notation as $= {}^{\mathrm{EL}}\!/_{M}$.

Marginal income theorem from increasing the discriminatory power of scoring

Let the CAP curve CAP(x, AR) have a single root $\tilde{x}(\mathrm{AR}) \in (0, 1)$ of the equation $\frac{\partial^2}{\partial x \partial \mathrm{AR}} \mathrm{CAP}(x, \mathrm{AR}) = 0$. If the business is guided by the goal of maximizing profit in its decision on the cut-off level, then there is a region in the parameter space $\beta > 0$, $\mathrm{AR} \in (0, 1)$, in which the annual return P from a marginal increase in the Gini index by $\Delta\mathrm{AR}$ will be estimated as follows:

$$P > \tilde{\pi} \cdot \Delta AR. \tag{9}$$

Where $\tilde{\pi} = \hat{E} \cdot \frac{EL}{2}$ this is a parameter for a loan portfolio with a constant amount $\hat{E}$.

In fact, this means that, given the amount of loans $\hat{E}$ (annual) and the level of expected average annual losses of applicants EL, for each percentage point of increase in

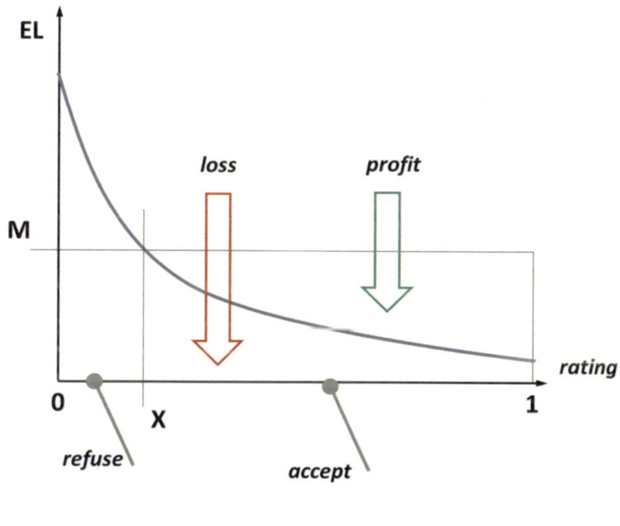

Figure 3.
The optimal point **X** *cut-off (cutting off "bad" from "good" borrowers) must correspond to the level of losses* EL(x) *that does not exceed the marginal return on the loan (margin* M*).*

[5] In addition to the lost profit, the loss from the deviation is assumed to be zero, although in practice this is not the case, since the "refuseniks" go through the process of internal underwriting, which is costly for the bank. These costs are a much smaller order of magnitude than credit losses, but in an accurate financial model, of course, should be taken into account.

the power of the rating system, there will be a guaranteed increase in profits of $\tilde{\pi} \cdot 0.01$ in the parameter space estimated in the next section. That is, given that provisions on placed loans (passed by risk management) may be less than the risks of the applicants, then for each percentage point increase in the risk management Gini index, the income level is estimated as half the volume of provisions multiplied by 0.01.

Proof

The total profit of the credit process will be determined by the formula (4):

$$\hat{\Pi} = M \cdot (1 - \hat{x} - \beta \cdot (1 - CAP(\hat{x},\ AR,\ p)), \tag{10}$$

where $\hat{x}$ – optimal cut-off point. Obviously, the point $\hat{x}$ will be calculated from the condition as follows:

$$\frac{\partial \Pi}{\partial x} = M \cdot (\beta \cdot CAP'_x(\hat{x},\ AR,\ p) - 1) = 0, \tag{11}$$

Which is equivalent to the identity $EL(\hat{x}) = M$ and corresponds **Figure 3**.

If the discrimination power AR is increased by a small amount ΔAR , then the formula for marginal income should be obtained from the expression:

$\Delta \Pi = \frac{d\hat{\Pi}}{dAR} \cdot \Delta AR + o(\Delta AR)$. From (10) follows that

$$\pi = \frac{d\hat{\Pi}}{dAR} = M \cdot \left(-\frac{d\hat{x}}{dAR} + \beta \cdot CAP'_x \cdot \frac{d\hat{x}}{dAR} \right) + \mathrm{EL} \cdot CAP'_{AR}(\hat{x}, AR, p).$$

The first part of this expression is equal to zero due to the condition (11), means remains as:

$$\pi = \mathrm{EL} \cdot CAP'_{AR}(\hat{x}, AR, p).$$

Taking into account the volumes of placed funds $\hat{E}$, which are less than potential ones by $1 - \hat{x}$, the resulting formula will be rewritten in the form as shown below:

$$\pi = \frac{\hat{E}}{1 - \hat{x}} \cdot \mathrm{EL} \cdot CAP'_{AR}(\hat{x}, AR, p). \tag{12}$$

To estimate the guaranteed value of the desired marginal profit π, it is necessary to carry out more transformations (12). Namely, if formula (7) is rewritten taking into account all arguments, $AR = \frac{2 \cdot \int_0^1 CAP(x,\ AR,\ p)dx - 1}{1-p}$,

Then, after differentiation with respect to AR, we get the identity as:

$\frac{2}{1-p} \cdot \int_0^1 CAP'_{AR}(x, AR, p)dx = 1$. Which can be used in formula (12) and it will be rewritten in the following form:

$$\pi = \hat{E} \cdot \frac{\mathrm{EL}}{2} \cdot \frac{1-p}{1-\hat{x}} \cdot \frac{CAP'_{AR}(\hat{x}, AR, p)}{\int_0^1 CAP'_{AR}(x, AR, p)dx}. \tag{13}$$

Taking into account the mean value theorem (for example, [18], Theorem 5.19.), we can state that there are closed subsets $\hat{x}$ of the interval [0,1] on which the function of the right fractional part of the expression: (13)

$$\frac{CAP'_{AR}(\hat{x}, AR, p)}{\int_0^1 CAP'_{AR}(x, AR, p)dx} \geq 1 \tag{14}$$

If we require a fairly simple property of the CAP-curve, namely that there be a unique root $\tilde{x}(AR) \in (0, 1)$ of equations $\frac{\partial^2}{\partial x \partial AR} CAP(x, AR) = 0$, then these subsets are the only segment[6] $[x_1, x_2] \in [0, 1]$.

Then, if $\hat{x} \in [x_1, x_2]$, then we get a guaranteed estimate as:

$$\pi \geq \hat{E} \cdot \frac{EL}{2} \cdot \frac{1-p}{1-\hat{x}}.$$

The cut-off level x̂ exceeds the default probability level p. Indeed, the optimal cut-off for an ideal model (AR = 1) should be at a minimum level of $\hat{x} = p$, in this case, $(1-p)/(1-\hat{x}) = 1$. For a real model, if it has $0 < AR < 1$, the cut-off level must be greater than for the ideal one equal to p, which means $(1-p)/(1-\hat{x}) > 1$. Therefore, it can be argued that the segment $[x_1, x_2]$ guaranteed level $\pi > \tilde{\pi}$ occurs when $\tilde{\pi} = \hat{E} \cdot \frac{EL}{2}$. ∎

4. The area of risk-return and the Gini index, in which the margin effect works

This section presents the result of modeling the marginal profit of a unit amount of placed funds $\hat{E}$ in relation to the marginal profit guaranteed by formula (9) using the Van der Burgt CAP-curve model (1).

We define the normalized marginal return from an increase in discriminatory power AR as the ratio $\pi/\tilde{\pi}$. The profitability level π is determined by formula (12), guaranteed by $\tilde{\pi}$ formula (9). In the Van der Burgt CAP-curve model, the function $k(AR, p)$ is implicitly defined (2). In addition, as it is easy to see, the condition of the Theorem on the existence of a unique root $\tilde{x}(AR) \in (0, 1)$ of equations $\frac{\partial^2}{\partial x \partial AR} CAP(x, AR) = 0$ is true. This means that there is a single segment belonging to the cut-off level of $[x_1, x_2] \in [0, 1]$, in which inequality (14) is satisfied and there is a connected domain of parameters in which the conservative estimate (9) is true. Let's show it.

The normalized marginal return will be calculated by the formula as shown below:

$$\pi/\tilde{\pi} = \frac{2 \cdot CAP'_k(\hat{x}, k, p)}{(1-\hat{x}) \cdot \frac{dAR}{dk}},$$

where $k(AR, p)$ is the solution of the transcendental equation (2). After simple transformations, the formula for the normalized marginal return for the model under consideration is obtained:

$$\pi/\tilde{\pi} = \frac{1-p}{1-\hat{x}} \cdot \frac{(\hat{x}-1) \cdot e^{-k(\hat{x}+1)} - \hat{x} \cdot e^{-k\hat{x}} + e^{-k}}{e^{-k} - \frac{(1-e^{-k})^2}{k^2}}.$$

---

[6] Obviously, the function $CAP'_{AR}(\hat{x}, AR, p)$ has zero values at the boundaries of the interval $\hat{x} \in [0,1]$, as well as the function $CAP(\hat{x}, AR, p) - \hat{x}$. Therefore, it is sufficient to have a unique extremum $\hat{x}$ of the function $CAP'_{AR}(\hat{x}, AR, p)$ for inequality (14) to give a unique segment $[x_1, x_2] \in [0, 1]$ as a solution.

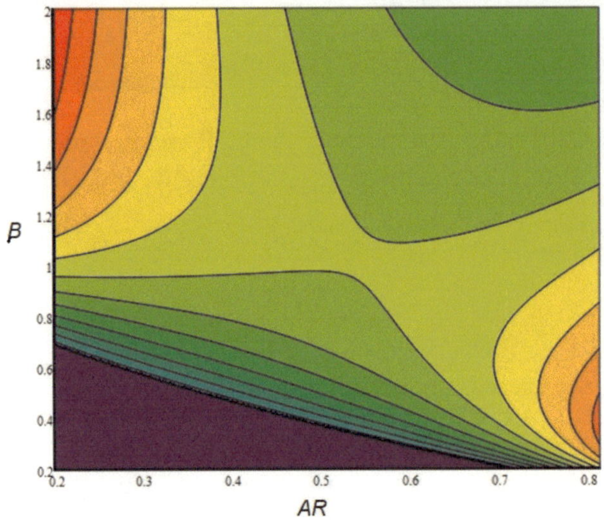

Figure 4.
Level lines of the normalized marginal return in the range of parameters $\in [0.2, 2]$, $\boldsymbol{AR} \in [0.2, 0.8]$. *In the blue area, the normalized marginal return does not reach unity (guaranteed return (9) is not achieved).*

Numerical study of the Van der Burgt CAP curve model for a realistic set of parameters $\frac{EL}{M} \in [0.2,2]$, $AR \in [0.2,0.8], p = 4\%$ (the influence of parameter p is small) presented in **Figure 4**.

Figure 4 shows the normalized marginal return level lines in a two-dimensional range of parameters. In the blue (close to triangular) area of low risk and the power of the rating system, the guaranteed marginal return is not achieved. In the upper part of the parameter area, the marginal return from improving the rating system already exceeds the guaranteed value by 2–3 times, especially in reddening zones.

The presented case shows the practical reliability of a conservative estimate of marginal return when the rating system is improved in the range of risk parameters that are most interesting for the use of rating models in decision making.

5. Results and discussion

Table 3 presents three common reasons for the weakness of discriminatory procedures in practice, for which hypotheses have been formed to improve their effectiveness. The formulation of these hypotheses, their development and increase in the effectiveness of risk management are the goals of its validation for the retail (including corporate) lending business.

The conservative marginal profit formula (9) gives the bank's management, without building complex financial business models, a conservative benchmark or tool that is the basis for making a decision to invest in their own risk management infrastructure to improve the efficiency of credit decision-making.[7] This also includes the decision to invest in the acquisition of third-party services that increase the effectiveness of risk management.

---

[7] By investment, here we mean the general regular and individual costs attributable to the cost of the business process.

Problem	Suggestions for solving the problem
Among the clients approved by the bank, a significant part leaves the offer unclaimed or goes to another bank. Those who use the offer turn out to be of lower quality than the average for approved ones. The result is a decrease in the Gini index.	Segment approved clients by credit quality, offering the best of them more favorable terms (Risk Based Pricing, RBP).
Reduced (increased) level of approval of applicants, decrease in the commercial effectiveness of the product due to the growth of type I or II errors.	Regular policy adjustments based on a request for market data (by market segment, by reference group) from the Credit Bureau. Adjusting the optimum failure rate to current rates.
Low discriminatory power of the lending process in certain segments. Result: zero Gini index, unreasonably high failure rate.	Refinement of scoring models, introduction of segment-oriented models, testing and validation of customized and (or) industry-specific scoring by the Credit Bureau.
Stagnation of the overall level of commercial efficiency of retail lending.	Regular validation of risk management procedures, scoring models, system of rules (stop factors), study of the behavior of "refuseniks". Implementation of motivational tools for risk managers and employees of lending departments to improve the efficiency of the lending process.

Table 3.
Typical reasons for risk management weakness.

Here are some simplified business cases:

- the bank intends to create a separate department that controls the quality of rating models, their validation, the quality of implementation and application in the business process. It is assumed that such a department will lead to an improvement in the discriminatory process by at least a 5% Gini index. Loan portfolio controlled by a discriminatory process based on rating modeling is **$10** billion, estimate of expected losses based on IFRS 9 provisions for the first stage of impairment[8] is **2**%. What budget of this business function will break even for the bank? Applying formula (9), we obtain only financial profit estimated at least **$10** billion $\cdot$ **2**%/**2** $\cdot$ **5**% = **$5** million annual. Nonfinancial profit is expressed in bullets 2–4 of Section 1;

- the bank understands that the quality of internal ratings is at an average level and is inferior to the quality of ratings provided by the services of a professional rating agency. Moreover, it is inferior, according to agreed estimates, by at least **10**% of the Gini index. The bank allows the involvement of an agency for a nonpublic rating of borrowers that are doubtful for the bank (legal aspects should be in the background and not discussed). The cut-off level of such applicants' projects is **50**%, the expected losses, as in the first case, are **2**%. The cost of the nonpublic rating service is **$3** thousand. Starting from what credit limit does it become profitable to involve the services of a rating agency, provided that the services are paid at the expense of the bank? A simple calculation using (9), considering the doubling of the cost, including for "refuseniks", gives a

[8] These are credit loans for which there are no clear signs of deterioration in credit quality yet. As a rule, all applicants, after making a decision on a loan, belong to the first stage of impairment.

conservative result $\$6$ thousand $\cdot 2/2\%/10\% = \$6$ million . That is, this is the limit, starting from which, it is advisable to attract a rating agency, and this limit can be proportionally reduced, taking into account lending for a period of more than one year, since the expected losses will increase proportionally (more precisely, almost proportionally).

In practice, decision-making problems are obviously more difficult. Since all related aspects must be considered, such as the incomplete "marketability" of proposed transactions, the quality of collateral and its assessment, data privacy factors, the target aspect of financing, control mechanisms, etc. However, this does not detract from the value of the fundamental profit assessment proposed by the developed approach.

Currently, there is a continuous improvement in scoring approaches to assess the applicant for loans. The methods use extended data, including nonfinancial data, which requires additional resources both to maintain significantly increased data volumes and to implement more complex algorithms and procedures. The payback of these resources for the credit business can be assessed by the above tools. According to the portfolio statistics of the decisions made, it is possible to objectively assess the current effectiveness of risk management. In [19], an overview of the areas of alternative credit scoring is presented. This field is emerging and gaining popularity due to the critical role of alternative data in accelerating access to financial services. Historically, a creditworthiness assessment has required the existence of past financial activity, such as repaying a loan. Such strict requirements made people with little or no financial history "credit invisible". Advances in artificial intelligence and machine learning have enabled scoring algorithms to work with nonfinancial data, such as digital footprints from mobile devices and psychometric data, to calculate credit scores. Although most invisible loans are in developing countries, research in this area is predominantly conducted in developed countries, and most alternative credit scoring models are trained on data from developed countries.

The study [20] explores the use of psychometric tests developed by the Entrepreneurial Finance Laboratory (EFL) as a tool to identify high credit risk and potentially increase access to credit for small business owners in Peru. Administrative data is used to compare accrual and repayment behavior patterns among entrepreneurs who have been offered credit based on the traditional credit rating method and the EFL tool. It has been found that a psychometric test can reduce the risk of a loan portfolio if it is used as a secondary screening mechanism for entrepreneurs already working in a bank, i.e. those who have a credit history. For nonbank entrepreneurs who do not have a credit history, using the EFL tool can increase access to credit without increasing portfolio risk. Another pilot project [21] to study the effectiveness of scoring based on psychometric data was launched in 2017 in Spain as part of the business microcredit segment (i.e. social microcredit for self-employed clients who want to start a business and need help from social organizations to develop your business plan). Initial statistical tests say that the discriminatory power (as measured by the Gini index of the ROC curve) can be in the range of 70-80% (compared to the 30–40% Gini index offered by traditional models). This means that the use of psychometric scoring can significantly increase the discriminating power and give a financial profit (9), which for the reference population of loan applicants should exceed the costs of introducing new risk management tools.

Another example of improving scoring power by expanding data coverage is a study [22] showing that adding social media-derived variables to a scorecard increases the Gini index by 7–8%.

And, of course, improving the scoring schemes themselves, considering the dynamics of scoring variables, and approaches that go beyond regression also show their increased discriminatory effectiveness. Yibei et al. [23] proposes a Bayesian optimal filter to provide risk prediction for lenders, assuming that published credit ratings are estimated simply from structured financial data. A recursive Bayesian scoring is proposed to improve the accuracy of credit scoring by incorporating a dynamic customer interaction topology. Theoretically, it is shown that, in accordance with the proposed concept of evolution, the developed scoring system has higher accuracy than any effective estimate, and the standard errors are strictly less than the lower Cramer-Rao bound in a certain range of scoring points. In [24], the approach of logistic regression is improved by introducing a new class of covariant categorization methods in regression models for binary response variables. Application to real data and Monte Carlo simulation study suggests that one of the methods of this class has better predictive performance and lower computational cost than other methods available in the literature.

6. Conclusion

This chapter presents a set of original tools that can be used in practice to improve the quality and efficiency of risk management for mass lending products (retail, microfinance, SME, and others). The first tool that is successfully used in the banking practice of the largest banks in Russia is the assessment of the effectiveness of credit decision-making in terms of discrimination of applicants for a loan. It relies on the generally accepted approach of ROC analysis. Measurement indicators are:

- assessment of the quasi-Gini indicator of the overall lending process, based on the decisions to reject and approve applicants;
- assessment of the scale of nonoptimality of the cut-off level of candidates, taking into account the current market risk-return of the segment of the population of candidates for bank clients.

Based on the results of measuring the effectiveness of risk management, it seems possible to give reasonable hypotheses for improving the business process in a given segment or proposals for restructuring or closing the direction.

The second tool is the rigorously proven Marginal income theorem (9) underscoring power amplification. Which gives a simple formula for the lower estimate of such income. The application of this formula can serve as a fundamental economic justification for the issue of allocating resources to improve scoring models, procedures, and the quality of risk management in general, depending on the current risk-return and discriminatory power. It is shown that the formula works in the most interesting areas for decision-making. Namely, when the risk/return of incoming candidates is greater than one and when the risk management in its decisions has a discriminating power that is much higher than random. Examples of consequences, hypotheses, and business cases are proposed. Also, a targeted overview of modern promising areas for improving the efficiency of risk management in terms of improving the accuracy of scoring models underlying credit business processes is given.

Author details

Mikhail Pomazanov
National Research University Higher School of Economics, Moscow,
Russian Federation

*Address all correspondence to: mhubble@yandex.ru

References

[1] Basel III. A Global Regulatory Framework for More Resilient Banks and Banking Systems. Basel Committee on Banking Supervision; 2011. pp. 1-77 . Available from: https://www.bis.org/publ/bcbs189.pdf [Accessed: August 01, 2022]

[2] ECB Guide to the internal capital adequacy assessment process (ICAAP). European Central Bank: Banking Supervision. 2018. pp. 1-45. Available from: https://www.bankingsupervision.europa.eu/ecb/pub/pdf/ssm.icaap_guide_201811.en.pdf [Accessed: August 01, 2022]

[3] Al Amari A. The credit evaluation process and the role of credit scoring: A case study of Qatar [Ph.D. thesis]. University College Dublin; 2002. pp. 1-387. Available from: https://books.google.ru/books?id=mXPjSAAACAAJ [Accessed: August 01, 2022]

[4] Abdou H, Pointon J. Credit scoring, statistical techniques and evaluation criteria: A review of the literature. Intelligent Systems in Accounting, Finance & Management. 2011;**18**(2–3): 59-88. DOI: 10.1002/isaf.325

[5] Rudra Kumar M, Kumar GV. Review of machine learning models for credit scoring analysis. Revista Ingeniería Solidaria. 2020;**16**(1):1-16. Available from: https://revistas.ucc.edu.co/index.php/in/article/view/3087. DOI: 10.16925/2357-6014.2020.01.11

[6] Jankowitsch R, Pichler S, Schwaiger Walter SA. Modelling the economic value of credit rating systems. Journal of Banking & Finance. 2007;**31-1**:181-198. DOI: 10.1016/j.jbankfin.2006.01.003

[7] Stein RM. The relationship between default prediction and lending profits: Integrating ROC analysis and loan pricing. Journal of Banking and Finance. 2005;**29**:1213-1236. DOI: 10.1016/j.jbankfin.2004.04.008

[8] Blöchlinger A, Leippold M. Economic benefit of powerful credit scoring. Journal of Banking and Finance. 2006; **30**:851-873. DOI: 10.1016/j.jbankfin.2005.07.014

[9] Engelmann B, Hayden E, Tasche D. Measuring the Discriminative Power of Rating Systems. Bundesbank Series 2 Discussion Paper2003. DOI: 10.2139/ssrn.2793951

[10] Joon-Ho H, Sangche L. Economic effects of positive credit information sharing: The case of Korea. Applied Economics. 2011;**43**:4879-4890. DOI: 10.1080/00036846.2010.498364

[11] Brian D, Claudia P, Troy R. Bigger is better, but at what cost? Estimating the economic value of incremental data assets. Big Data. 2014;**2**:87-96. DOI: 10.1089/big.2014.0010

[12] Chen Y, Chen S, Chen Y. Decision quality by the loss cost of type I and type II errors. The TQM Journal. 2013;**25**(2): 202-220. DOI: 10.1108/17542731311299627

[13] Pomazanov MV. Validation of the effectiveness of the bank retail portfolio risk management procedure. Procedia Computer Science. 2022;**199**:798-805. DOI: 10.1016/j.procs.2022.01.099

[14] van der Burgt M. Calibrating low-default portfolios, using the cumulative accuracy profile. The Journal of Risk Model Validation. 2008;**1**:17-33. DOI: 10.21314/JRMV.2008.016

[15] Birdsall TG. The Theory of Signal Detectability: ROC Curves and their Character. In: Cooley Electronics

Laboratory. Ann Arbor, Michigan: Department of Electrical and Computer Engineering, The University of Michigan; 1966. p. 451. Available from: https://hdl.handle.net/2027.42/3618 [Accessed: August 01, 2022]

[16] Hanley JA. Receiver operating characteristic (ROC) methodology: The state of the art. Critical Reviews in Diagnostic Imaging. 1989;**29**(3):307-335

[17] Tasche D. Estimating Discriminatory Power and PD Curves When the Number of Defaults Is Small. Working Paper. Lloyds Banking Group; 2009. Available from: https://arxiv.org/abs/0905.3928 [Accessed: August 01, 2022]

[18] Rudin W. Principles of Mathematical Analysis. 3rd ed. New York: McGraw-Hill; 1976. p. 113. ISBN 978-0-07-054235-8

[19] Njuguna R, Sowon K. Poster: A scoping review of alternative credit scoring literature. In: ACM SIGCAS Conference on Computing and Sustainable Societies (COMPASS '21). New York, USA: Association for Computing Machinery; 2021. pp. 437-444. DOI: 10.1145/3460112.3471972

[20] Arráiz I, Bruhn M, Stucchi R. Psychometrics as a Tool to Improve Screening and Access to Credit Policy Research Working Paper. Washington, DC: World Bank; 2015. Available from: https://openknowledge.worldbank.org/handle/10986/23471 [Accessed: August 01, 2022]

[21] Microbank's pilot on psychometric scoring. European Microfinance Network (EMN). 2018. Available from: https://www.european-microfinance.org/publication/microbanks-pilot-psychometric-scoring [Accessed: August 01, 2022]

[22] Masyutin AA. Credit scoring based on social network data. Business Informatics. 2015;**3**(33):15-23. Available from: http://cyberleninka.ru/article/n/credit-scoring-based-on-social-network-data [Accessed: August 01, 2022]

[23] Yibei L, Ximei W, Boualem D, Xiaoming H. Credit scoring by incorporating dynamic networked information. European Journal of Operational Research. 2020;**286**(3):1103-1112. DOI: 10.1016/j.ejor.2020.03.078

[24] Silva D, Pereira G, Magalhães T. A class of categorization methods for credit scoring models. European Journal of Operational Research. 2022;**296-1**:323-331. DOI: 10.1016/j.ejor.2021.04.029